STRATEGIC ECONOMY IN JAPAN

Thomas M. Huber

WESTVIEW PRESS
Boulder • San Francisco • Oxford

Published in 1994 in the United States of America by Westview Press, Inc., 5500 Central Avenue, Boulder, Colorado 80301-2877, and in the United Kingdom by Westview Press, 36 Lonsdale Road, Summertown, Oxford OX2 7EW

Library of Congress Cataloging-in-Publication Data
Huber, Thomas M.
  Strategic economy in Japan / Thomas M. Huber.
    p.   cm.
Includes bibliographical references (p.   ) and index.
  ISBN 0-8133-2092-5 — ISBN 0-8133-2095-X (pbk.)
  1. Japan—Economic policy—1989–   2. Industry and state—Japan.
I. Title.
HC462.95.H84   1994
338.952—dc20   93-43012
                                                                              CIP

Printed and bound in the United States of America

 The paper used in this publication meets the requirements
of the American National Standard for Permanence of Paper
for Printed Library Materials Z39.48-1984.

10   9   8   7   6   5   4   3   2   1

Contents

Tables and Figures

Acknowledgments

I WISH TO THANK those who provided inspiration and confidence when I first began my study of strategic institutions, especially Denny, Roger, Jack, and George. I am also grateful to my colleagues for their generous encouragement and frequent advice when I was exploring the nature of strategic institutions in the early days—Chris, George, Sam, and all the others. My students, too, by years of patient toil, have helped me to see more clearly, and I am grateful especially to Mark's people for their elan and supportive spirit. Many useful suggestions for this text were offered by friends who were kind enough to read the manuscript, especially Chalmers and Bob.

Needless to say, the opinions and perspectives presented in this volume are those of myself alone, not of individuals mentioned here or of any institutions with which I have been affiliated. The views expressed in this book do not reflect the official policy or position of the Department of the Army, the Department of Defense, or the U.S. government.

Thomas M. Huber

Introduction

JAPAN'S ECONOMIC PERFORMANCE in the postwar era has commonly been described as miraculous. Japan's extraordinary sustained growth has not been matched by any other major nation in modern history. Between 1952 and 1973, the Japanese economy grew at an average rate of nearly 10 percent per year. As a consequence, Japan's gross domestic product (GDP) was more than six times as large in 1973 as it had been in 1952. By the end of this period Japan had the world's second largest economy after the United States. In 1978 it would also pass the United States to become first in per capita production.[1] By 1973 Japan was first in steel, ships, electronics, and optics. Later it would become first in autos, semiconductors, computers, and robotics as well. Moreover, by the mid-1960s, after 10 years of rapid growth, illiteracy, poverty, and unemployment had virtually disappeared from the society.

Fortunately in recent decades new scholarship has emerged from many quarters that has begun to make it possible to achieve a more fundamental understanding of some aspects of the Japanese miracle. A consensus has begun to take shape among students of government and of commercial institutions—namely political scientists and scholars associated with business schools—that although Japan enjoys a vigorous private commerce, at the same time the Japanese government is somehow a participant in Japan's techno-industrial system. The system seems to have the benefit of some kind of business-government partnership. My purpose here is to further this collective pursuit of understanding in some small way by bringing some of this new scholarship together, and also by exploring Japan's distinctive economic arrangements in light of public institutional practices in the West, rather than exclusively in light of private commercial practices. This approach in itself is not new, of course, insofar as earlier observers have from time to time pointed out the similarity of certain Japanese economic practices to those of public institutions in the West.[2]

For want of a better term, I will refer to the distinctive Japanese system, in which certain elements of the economy may have been brought under public sponsorship, as "strategic economy." Conceptual insights into Japanese techno-

1

industrial practices can be achieved by analogy to academic, ecclesiastic, diplomatic, and other public institutions in the West. Still, the most useful environments of reference may be those of public institutions that are normally guided by a national strategy, especially military institutions.

The first chapter of this study seeks to concisely describe how economic policy is made and by whom. It recounts the means by which Japan's elite bureaucracy coordinates Japanese industry and the limits of this coordination, its objectives, and some unexpected advantages. Chapter 2 explores the structure and respective purposes of institutions at the intermediate levels of coordination-by-direct-instruction in the Japanese system: neo-zaibatsu, industrial associations, and cartels. This chapter also explains the Ministry of International Trade and Industry's (MITI) occasional restructuring of these institutions to improve their effect. Chapter 3 sheds light on institutions at intermediate levels that influence techno-industrial activity by regulating the flow of funds and materials in ways that conform to the normal functioning of markets. A fourth chapter describes the lower levels of coordination in the Japanese system, namely strategic corporations and their affiliated firms. In other words, these opening chapters represent an effort to analyze the several functional levels of Japan's domestic economic strategy. Chapter 5 offers insights into the structures of implementation of Japan's international economic strategy. Chapter 6 sounds out the objectives of the international strategy and explores Japan's strategic economic activity abroad. The final chapter is an attempt to achieve further insights into Japan's strategic economy by examining it with reference to several Western scholarly and historical perspectives.

NOTES

1. Organization for Economic Cooperation and Development, *The Industrial Policy of Japan* (Paris: OECD, 1972) [hereafter OECD], p. 163. For industrial growth rates see Chalmers Johnson, *MITI and the Japanese Miracle* (Stanford, CA: Stanford University Press, 1982), pp. 4–5. For per capita GNP, see, for example, Ezra F. Vogel, *Japan as Number One* (New York: Harper and Row, 1979), p. 21.

2. For this notion, cf. Ronald Dore, *British Factory–Japanese Factory* (Berkeley: University of California Press, 1973), pp. 275–76; Clyde V. Prestowitz, *Trading Places* (New York: Basic Books, 1988), p. 156.

PART ONE

DOMESTIC STRATEGY

1
MITI: Prospero's World

T HE TECHNO-INDUSTRIAL SECTORS of the Japanese economy appear to operate on principles of national well-being and security, somewhat in the manner of a modern strategic military or foreign policy system. Let us consider in brief how strategic-economic policy decisions are made, the methods by which such policies are implemented, and the objectives usually sought and achieved by these systems.

Making Policy: The Ministry of International Trade and Industry

Economic policy in Japan appears to be formulated initially by the elite bureaucracy, not by the elected National Diet. Policies relating to strategic industries are both fashioned and implemented by the Ministry of International Trade and Industry (MITI). MITI is possibly the most powerful institution politically, economically, and socially in Japanese society. Its several hundred senior operatives chart the future of Japan, Incorporated.[1]

MITI officials do not shape policies in a void. They consult a senior advisory board called the Industrial Structure Council (ISC). The ISC consists of some 130 members—serving two-year terms—drawn from industry, finance, academia, and government. The council's chairman is the current chief of the powerful industrial umbrella association the Keidanren. The ISC is subdivided into industry-specific councils that issue a steady stream of white papers for their industries, appropriately called "visions." In fact, however, ISC staff support is provided entirely by MITI, and the ISC is evidently cued by MITI as to the directions in which industry should move. It is likely that part of the ISC's function is to serve as a microcosm of the interested public constituencies so that MITI can gauge the response, and cull the insights, of these constituencies in a manageable way. A cabinet-level structure called the Economic Planning Agency (EPA) also generates long-term advisory perspectives for the economy.[2]

MITI drafts five-year plans for economic growth based on ISC and EPA perspectives, as well as on estimates of the general tenor of public opinion. The typical objective of the five-year plans is to achieve rapid doubling or quadrupling of selected industrial categories such as metals, shipbuilding, electronics, automotives, or the like. To succeed, the plans must precisely synchronize the increased availability of every production factor: capital, skilled technicians, raw materials, construction assets, product and process technology, producers' durables, transport for materials and products, and markets for the product. In most cases this planning involves global as well as domestic coordination. The most famous of the postwar economic plans is the National Income Doubling Plan of 1960, which aimed to, and did, double Japan's gross domestic product (GDP) in seven years. Other plans adopted by MITI during the period of rapid growth, 1952 to 1973, included the Five Year Plan for Economic Development (initiated 1955), the New Long Term Economic Plan (1957), the Middle Term Economic Plan (1965), and the Economic and Social Development Plan (1967).[3]

In practice the five-year plans are in the nature of an overarching policy framework and are constantly scrutinized, sometimes undergoing major revisions before their term. Thus a given plan may not last for five years. Moreover, in accordance with the economic plans' prescriptions, each bureau in MITI generates specific medium-term plans, called "elevation plans." This is done in close consultation with several constituencies, including officials of the corporations that will ultimately have to implement them. These plans indicate amounts to be spent for research and development, proportion of production to be exported, and much more. They provide for a two- or three-year interval rather than the five or so years of the typical ministrywide plan. In other words, the bureau plans narrow the focus of the ministrywide plan in terms of both the time interval and the industrial area covered. They give a more specific reality to the ministry's (and society's) more abstract objectives.[4]

MITI's authority to make and implement economic plans derives from legislation passed by the Japanese National Diet. MITI bureau staffs draft enabling legislation for MITI's programs. The MITI career deputy minister takes these drafts to a meeting of deputy ministers that is convened prior to legislation being submitted to the Diet. To go forward, MITI must persuade the other ministries' representatives that the legislation is desirable. If the deputy ministers approve the proposals, they then go to the Diet, which usually votes them into law. It is probably fair to say that 90 percent of legislation that is passed is generated by the elite ministries. The Diet has very little staff with which to generate or evaluate legislation. Only the elite bureaus have this capacity in abundance. Let us explore this pattern a bit further.

Bureaucratic Legislation: Parliamentary Review

Recent Western observers have called Japan's system of government an enigma, perhaps with good reason.[5] Japanese legislative patterns, at least where economic matters are concerned, are rather different from those in the United States. In Japan a meritocratic body of legal experts, the elite ministries, generates the legislation with its staffs, and the elective National Diet is then free to pass the legislation or not.[6] In other words, the Diet receives and reviews the legislation drafted by the bureaucracy and ordinarily passes it. Having little staff support, the Diet may not be able to do much more. Japanese democratic practice, at least in economic matters, might be described as bureaucratic legislation with parliamentary review, a pattern somewhat different from what Anglo-Americans might usually expect.[7]

Moreover, laws that the National Diet passes, in economic as in other fields, represent a broad mandate, not specific prescriptions, thus giving the ministries an additional quasi-legislative power. The same elite bureaus that enforce the laws (and draft them) also interpret and give specificity to them in the form of numerous ordinances that the bureaus issue on their own authority and that they may alter or elaborate at will. Implementing the 1984 Telecommunications Business Law required 67 ministerial ordinances, for example. If the bureaus do not exercise their ordinance authority appropriately, the Diet is free to revoke it. The Diet does not ordinarily presume to meddle with the ordinances, however. Diet representatives apparently believe that fine adjustments in the regulations are best made by the officials closest to implementation and that having to seek Diet approval for every small change would lead to a needless and imprudent rigidity. Economic legislation is also coordinated by industry-specific committees of the influential Liberal Democratic Party (LDP), which correspond to MITI's industry-specific bureaus.[8]

Beyond that, economic policy is scrutinized by the press corps, which does introduce a robust democratic element into the process. The press is expected to air the public's views on economic policy and to participate in a substantial way in policy formation and is entirely free to do this. Once a policy is fixed, however, the press is expected to support its implementation and is subjected to some constraints in that regard akin to Western constraints on press reporting of military operations. The government provides information only to members of the Press Club, which is divided by ministry. That is, each major newspaper has several reporters that specialize in MITI-related news. MITI routinely gives the newspapers the information they want but also expects them to refrain from printing certain information that is sensitive. In other words, Japan's economic officials expect, and tacitly require, the Japanese press to cooperate where policy implementation is concerned. Reporters mainly do so, partly because they do share MITI's goals of national enrichment and partly because they could lose their all-important Press Club credentials.[9] The consequence, in any case, is that there is vigorous debate over policy formation but relatively little independent reporting of policy implementation by these reporters. In fact, both press and Diet seem to be dependent on MITI staffs for their information about actual policy operation.

Strategic Policy and Democracy

What all of this means is that MITI makes economic policy, but while doing so it is intensely scrutinized by the public, the press, and the Diet. The elite bureau drafts the legislation but beyond that there are several democratic dynamics in play. Opposition parties in the Diet especially are likely often to publicly challenge MITI proposals. Policies are bureaucratically made, but at the same time any major changes in policy must constantly confront public opinion. In practice MITI must act not only in the public interest but also in ways the public perceives as being in its interest. MITI shapes policy, but other ministries, political parties, and the press have de jure or de facto power to veto or weaken MITI's policies.

Are all these doings completely strange and incomprehensible to Americans? Not necessarily. Japanese economic policies are bureaucratically made but are nonetheless exposed to public opinion. In short, Japanese economic policy is formulated much as defense policy or foreign policy is usually formulated in the United States: by career professionals for the public. U.S. career officers in the military or State Department devise plans, both general and specific, that congressional committees then scrutinize, and if the plans are in accord with prevailing public opinion, they are usually accepted. All this is done in a constant flurry of journalistic commentary and public debate. In Japan, strategic plans for the economy are generated by high-ranking economic officials amidst a flurry of journalistic debate and are usually approved by the people's representatives if they are in accord with public opinion.[10]

The Japanese pattern of bureaus draft, Diet reviews, bureaus implement is different from the usual U.S. practice of Congress drafts, Court reviews, bureaus implement. The instructive U.S. exception, of course, is in areas of strategic importance that "provide for the common defense." In a social consensus older than the republic, the U.S. tradition is to place responsibility for operational decisions in the hands of its highest military officers. When Washington became commander in chief of the Continental armies in the summer of 1775, the society viewed this as a normal and appropriate way to proceed. Legislators advised their commanders of the basic objectives to be achieved, gave them the resources, and left the matter to them. The reason was that if Washington had to get Congress's approval for every move he made, his campaign would be brought to a halt. In an active strategic environment, it was not normally in the interest of the Congress or people to intervene in the efforts of their best commanders.

In strategic areas, namely military areas, U.S. constitutional practice, from Washington's day to ours, has been to place exceptional authority—one might fairly say quasi-legislative authority—in its officer corps. This authority includes forming and reforming force structure and creating the regulations that govern the force, a quasi-legislative authority over which Congress exercises what amounts to a power of review. The officer corps that enforces the regulations also drafts them and adjudicates them. Where vital security interests are at stake, Congress has entrusted vast wealth and human resources to this body of professional officers. Moreover, citizens and enlistees are expected to support military activities out of shared patriotic concerns.

The U.S. military is constrained by a sophisticated system of checks and compromises calculated to allow it to be effective yet not jeopardize the democratic spirit of the society in general. Military authority is great, but delimited. It does not extend into the society; it is subordinated to civilian command authority, dependent on legislated budgeting, scrutinized by the press, and the like. The U.S. press is free to debate military policies, but when covering war, like the Japanese economic press covering implementation, is held to a more stringent standard. Although free, it is expected to report in ways compatible with the operational and public interest; for example, it must not divulge surprise attacks or report names of combat victims before the families are informed.

Over time the remarkable role of the officer corps has become steadily more pronounced as military affairs have grown in scale and technical complexity. Once Congress indicates essential national security objectives, military general staffs draw and redraw long-term and short-term defense plans, which are translated into specific operational prescriptions at successively lower staff levels. Congressional staffers who fully understand the proposals the military brings before congressional committees for approval are few and treasured. Congress continues to authorize this esoteric military activity at some appropriate level, provided it believes the activity actually is effective in achieving essential national security objectives. In strategic matters, the Pentagon drafts and the Congress reviews.

U.S. and Japanese political traditions are in some respects very different. In spite of this, there appear to be significant parallels in some of the dynamics of policy formation between the Japanese strategic economy and the U.S. military system.[11] Is this just a historical accident? Perhaps; the other possibility is that these institutional arrangements are highly advantageous for modern strategic effectiveness and therefore, once discovered, exert compelling appeal in strategic matters, no matter what the flavor of one's particular tradition might be.

Implementation: Three Methods

The techno-industrial sectors of Japan's economy may not only represent what we think of as a commercial system; they may also constitute a kind of strategic system serving national policy goals. We have seen how Japan's economic policy goals are established. Let us consider now the structure and dynamics by which policy is implemented. MITI has three principal modes of implementation: direct instruction to industrial institutions regarding strategic objectives (a kind of non-interventionist command), orchestration of the flow of major funds, and orchestration of the flow of certain materials. (MITI also has innumerable lesser holds over industry, several of which will be discussed in subsequent chapters.)

Direct instruction is not exactly command, but for some purposes it resembles command. In the postwar period, MITI, with the Ministry of Finance (hereafter MOF) and other ministries, has such substantially complete control over investment capital, taxes, technical standards, new technologies, and raw materials that even the appearance of noncompliance could have unwanted consequences for corporations that seem to be dallying. In other words, MITI appears to have something resembling command authority as a consequence of its other statutory leverages.

This quasi-command relationship in any case seems to rest lightly on the industries, in part because MITI informs companies of their objectives, then leaves them free to pursue them. Acceptance by industry is also due in part to the sophisticated arrangement between government and industry whereby middle levels of decisionmaking, between government and industry, are all staffed by the industries, not government, thus further shielding the corporations themselves from direct government intervention in practical operations.

Besides this, it is assumed that MITI will provide ample resources for anything it asks the industries to do and that this system will generate a bonanza of wealth for almost all of the managerial and labor groups involved. Companies involved in this wealth-generating activity are rewarded with extravagant and continuous prosperity. Corporations do not have much leeway for resisting MITI, and besides that they do not have much reason to do so.

Although these dynamics could be referred to as noninterventionist command or quasi-command, they could also be referred to by such terms as coordination and control, or simply direct instruction. The essence of this is merely that each corporation is informed of the particular role it must play both individually and in terms of the whole system in order to enjoy enormous strategic advantages. One of the ways MITI gets what it wants is through the deliberate, purposive action of industrial participants at all levels. So MITI advises, if need be on occasion more than advises, participants just below it of what each's role is and how that role relates to the roles of others and to the shared goal.

In the domain of direct strategic instruction, MITI works through three types of middle-level institution: neo-zaibatsu, industrial associations, and cartels. Which of these MITI works through depends on the kind of task it is trying to carry out. Let us consider the respective characteristics of these organizations in the Japanese system.

Direct Instruction: Neo-Zaibatsu

The neo-zaibatsu is an industrial task group called *keiretsu* in today's Japanese. There are six of these groups. Systematic diversity is their strength. They are especially useful to MITI in projects where a number of different industries must cooperate closely. Each neo-zaibatsu has one or several companies in each major industrial category—banking, heavy industry, steel, construction, and so on—so that each has universal capability for expansion projects. If it wishes to double steel production, the neo-zaibatsu already has the capital, the construction assets, the makers of production machinery, and most of the other necessary factors already available in-house. A wide diversity of institutional means allows the neo-zaibatsu to achieve complex strategic goals with relative ease. This diversity also allows member companies to accommodate each other in their daily operations as reliable consumers of each other's output. The whole task group of 20 to 40 companies then competes with other task groups. That is, they compete at cooperation for rapid growth.

The function of the neo-zaibatsu is conceptually somewhat analogous to that of a unified command in the U.S. military, for example Pacific Command (see Figure 1.1). Military operations in the Pacific are likely to require cooperative action by naval, air force, and ground units. Therefore there is a permanent command structure in Honolulu that has component commands from each service. Institutional diversity is the key to the effectiveness of the unified commands, and the reason for their existence. Five unified commands span the globe, and, like the neo-zaibatsu, they are a mechanism to ensure smooth cooperation among diverse assets.

The six neo-zaibatsu are Mitsubishi, Mitsui, Sumitomo, Fuyo (formerly Yasuda), Sanwa, and Daiichi (formerly Shibusawa and other concerns). Mitsubishi, with its three-diamond mark, is perhaps the best known. It includes 28 core companies. For financing it has the Mitsubishi Bank, Mitsubishi Trust, Meiji Life Insurance Company, and Tokio (sic) Fire and Marine Insurance Company. Its overseas arm is the general trading company Mitsubishi Corporation. The Mitsubishi group has five assorted chemical companies, a steel company, and an aluminum company, not to mention Mitsubishi Motors, Japan Optics (Nikon), and Mitsubishi Heavy Industries.[12]

The neo-zaibatsu bank always supervises and funds the other enterprises and is the first among equals. MITI officials may guide neo-zaibatsu conduct either by contacting the chief executives of the bank or by contacting chief executives of the individual firms. This kind of activity is possible because external private stockholders in strategic firms are effectively disassociated from policymaking, which is thus influenced only by the long-term institutional and national goals of management or the government. Thus the existence of the neo-zaibatsu allows MITI officials to mobilize vast institutional resources with relatively little effort. In

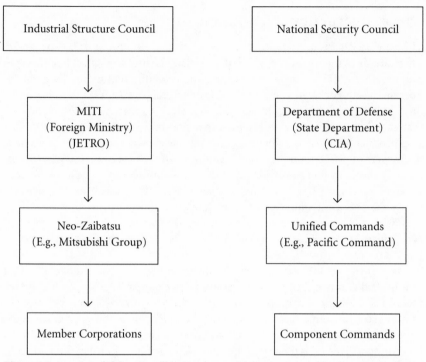

Figure 1.1 *Routing of Policy Coordination Among Major Agencies of the Japanese Economy and of the U.S. Military*

other words, the neo-zaibatsu function rather like what the military calls an intermediate echelon of command.

Industrial Associations and Cartels

Besides instructing producers directly through neo-zaibatsu groups, MITI exercises its direct coordination function through industrial associations and temporary ad hoc groups called cartels (see Figure 1.2). Industrial associations are mainly used for objectives that affect all or part of a single industry, such as quality control, the proliferation of a new technology, or growth or shrinkage of a whole industry. Neo-zaibatsu are used mainly for objectives that require cooperation across industrial lines, including again the growth or shrinkage of a particular industry. In short, industrial associations are used to expedite coordination and cooperation within a single industry, and neo-zaibatsu are used to expedite cooperation among different industries. Both are important for the strategic

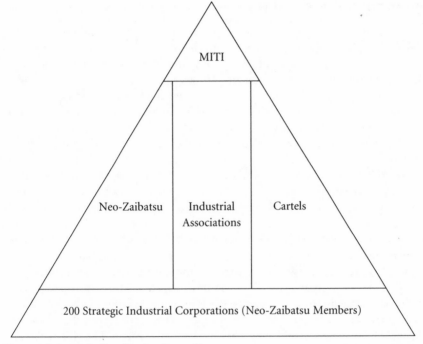

Figure 1.2 *Strategic Coordination Pyramid*

goals of rapid growth. Both industrial associations and neo-zaibatsu serve to mediate between the government and a large number of strategic manufacturing corporations. In this sense, both function as what the military calls an intermediate echelon of command.

Each major industry, such as steel or electrical machinery, has its own industrial association with a prominent firm president as the association president. The associations are integrated upward in the Federation of Economic Organizations, Keidanren. Industrial associations are also subdivided downward into branch associations for the major divisions of each industry, types of steel, and so on.[13]

Cartels differ from both neo-zaibatsu and industrial associations in that they are set up for a particular purpose, are often temporary, and involve an association of firms that are not expected to work together for purposes other than that for which the cartel was created. They are like a military task force, put together for a particular mission and dismantled when it is done. Cartels are like neo-zaibatsu and industrial associations, however, in that they are another institutional route by which MITI intentions are efficiently transmitted to industry.[14]

Planning: Ends and Means

Critics of economic planning often focus on cases in which planning has failed, such as the planning efforts of the recently defunct Soviet Union. Planning generally fails, critics correctly point out, because it replaces competition with a rigid mandate from above and micromanages lower levels of enterprise, thus stifling initiative. The Soviet Russian government intervened in all aspects of the economy at all levels to set both ends and means. It did indeed micromanage. It failed.

Planning in the Japanese case, however, has had far happier consequences than its Soviet counterpart. This may be because Japanese planning is fundamentally different from the Soviet sort: It is carefully limited and flexibly pluralistic, and there are whole zones of the economy where planning has no direct play at all. The Japanese government intervenes in the economy only to set ends, never to dictate means. Industries are completely free to implement policies as they wish. The government intervenes only at the top and respects the chain of command. This is possible because discipline at lower levels is ensured by competition, so the government does not have to micromanage. The government does intervene, however, to restructure whole industries to make sure there are a half-dozen viable enterprises competing in any given field, which are then completely free to grow or decline on their own merits. Government intervenes in the structures to perpetuate an environment of the most vigorous competition possible. Ezra Vogel likens the Japanese system to the National Football League. The NFL will cheerfully create or disband a team but will never presume to call the plays.[15] A robust competitive pluralism is compulsory in the Japanese system. Competition is not in spite of the planning; it is the purpose of the planning.

This arrangement, namely setting the ends at the top but having efficiency of means accomplished by competition, not command, at the bottom has a striking advantage: It fully preserves the benefits of spontaneity and freedom at the bottom of the system while retaining the advantages of coordination and united purpose at the top. It thus achieves the best of planned and free-market systems simultaneously, which makes for exceptional dynamism.

The Limits of Strategic Economy: Mundane Economy

Part of the genius of Japanese planning lies in its limits. Aspects of the Japanese economy that have no public or strategic importance are not orchestrated by the government at all. As a rule of thumb, strategic corporations probably own about one-fourth of the economy's assets, and influence, through stock ownership, perhaps an additional one-fourth. This means that from one-half to three-quarters of the economy lies outside the strategic coordination system altogether. Small retailers, small manufacturers, small restaurateurs, and the like are left entirely alone. The lunch counter at the gate of a U.S. Air Force base is not controlled by the U.S. Air Force. The noodle shop at the Mitsubishi plant gate is not controlled by Mitsubishi. The government practices laissez-faire toward the mundane consumer economy, except, of course, to constantly draw funds from it for the favored sectors of the strategic economy.

Tapping the mundane consumer economy for the sake of the strategic economy gives these two sectors very different wealth levels. Japan is therefore sometimes referred to as a "dual economy." The consumer economy is constantly drawn back to a state of material austerity by three methods whereby capital is perpetually withdrawn from it: dual credit, dual taxation, and dual pricing. Of course, this portion of the economy seems to flourish colorfully nonetheless.

This work is concerned mainly with the strategic economy, not the mundane economy. For those who wish to pursue it, however, there are many manifestations of this dichotomy both in Western scholarship and in Japanese institutional practice. There are about 200 companies that have an interlocking stock-ownership relation with neo-zaibatsu banks. Each of these has 11 to 200 affiliated client companies, according to T. J. Pempel.[16] All of these together, perhaps some 10,000 firms, constitute the strategic part of the economy. All the rest of Japan's approximately 1.7 million corporations and 11 million small businesses of all sorts are part of the quotidien consumer economy and have almost no strategic role.[17] They are smaller firms, sometimes very small, with few employees and little equipment.

These firms belong to the Japan Chamber of Commerce and Industry (JCCI), not the prestigious Keidanren.[18] They are under the jurisdiction of MITI's Small and Medium Enterprise Agency and not MITI's high-powered industrial bureaus. They are regulated by the Small and Medium Enterprise Fundamental Law and dozens of other Small and Medium laws, not the heavy industry and technology laws.[19] Scholars such as Yasukichi Yasuba have brought us useful insights into the "dualistic structure in postwar Japan," and the noteworthy "difference in wages, productivity, and technology between big and small businesses."[20]

There are many advantages to MITI's practice of leaving these small enterprises alone, among them being that there is no supervision cost and that supervising so many small units is impractical. Moreover, whether intended or not, this practice preserves a zone in the economy that is free of government guidance, where a free spirit, and freer spirits, can still thrive despite the discipline required in the strategic industrial sectors. It is a kind of safety valve for the society that guarantees that the spontaneity of the people and culture are sustained despite the demands of the industrial program.

Orchestration of Major Capital Flows: Financial Institutions

MITI, and in this case MOF, also shapes the Japanese economy by determining the flow of major capital funds. This is achieved primarily through the banking system but also by reliance on the Postal Savings System (PSS), neo-zaibatsu–linked insurance companies, and the tax system. The most essential mechanism of governance, however, is the Bank of Japan (BOJ) and the practices surrounding it. Japan's 120 million population and myriad small businesses are induced by various incentives to save a large proportion of their income and to place these savings in the 12 city banks, the Postal Savings System, the 64 regional banks, or insurance policies. The BOJ then sees to it that these funds make their way to promising MITI-sanctioned strategic industries. The system gathers saved funds from millions of households and small businesses and channels them to favored industries. To further accommodate priority industries, interest rates to them are set especially low, below the market rate.[21] The effect of all this is that resources are drawn from economic activities in the everyday, mundane areas of the economy so that strategic industrial growth may be invigorated.

Orchestration of Materials Flow: The Quasi-Private Monopoly

MITI is able to influence Japanese economic activity by determining the prices and distribution of certain important materials and manufactured goods. The object of this is sometimes to keep the prices of raw materials to producers down, sometimes to keep the prices to producers for their manufactured goods up, and sometimes to raise prices on nonstrategic goods such as sugar to generate revenue to cover these and other subsidies. There are scores of public policy companies (PPCs) involved in regulation of price and distribution of goods. Their mandates are set in general terms by MITI or by some other ministry they may be affiliated with. They operate otherwise, however, as autonomous corporations in the market. They are often empowered by law to buy all of a commodity produced from producers and to sell all of a commodity to be consumed to consumers. They are legal monopolies. They can set prices for the same reason private monopolists can: They dispose of all the product. They can do this with a minimum of disruption of markets because they are "market conforming." They mimic conventional market participants. They do not try to suspend or discourage market activity. They merely adjust the terms for some of that activity to accommodate strategic policy goals. Planners set certain parameters in the market by relying on PPCs. They then rely on a vigorous market to generate the consequences that they intend when they set those parameters. They never abridge the functioning of the market.[22]

Market Conformity

Japanese planners cherish the market. They intervene in the market, but they do so in ways that emulate normal market participants. They can thus influence the market without disrupting its normal functioning. Planners act by setting the conditions that operate in the market, not by suppressing the market or asking anyone to ignore the market. The advantage of this approach is that it preserves the dynamism and energy of persons or institutions seeking to enrich themselves in the market. Beyond that, the market is a superb tool that can do some things better than any other arrangement can. Above all, it is useful to achieve many complex, finely discriminated allocational decisions with virtually no supervisory or administrative costs. Chalmers Johnson refers to this kind of planning activity, working with the market rather than against it, as "market conforming methods."[23]

Three Methods of Implementation

The Japanese government thus operates Japan's strategic economy in three ways: (1) MITI and other ministries have what amounts to a strategic coordination relationship to neo-zaibatsu, industrywide associations, and cartels; (2) MOF and other ministries determine interest rates and large-scale flows of capital, that is, MOF determines the price and flow of money; and (3) the public policy companies (answerable to MITI, MOF, and other ministries) determine the price and distribution of certain important commodities (see Figure 1.3). These three methods might be thought of as roughly analogous to the steering wheel, accelerator, and carburetor of an automobile. Any of these devices alone is not sufficient to operate the vehicle. Together they provide smooth acceleration and cruising to the desired goal. MITI provides guidance, then also provides the means, the surge of energy that makes brisk movement possible.

The Genius of Limits

The Japanese techno-industrial system seems to have a number of attributes in common with modern strategic military systems in the West, especially in its upper coordinating levels. Like modern democratic military systems, much of its so-

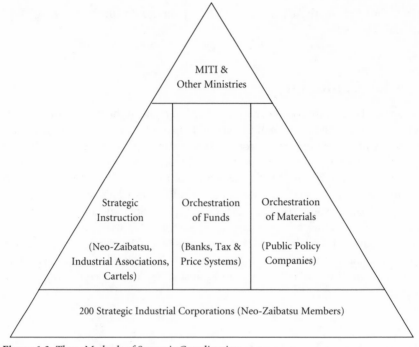

Figure 1.3 *Three Methods of Strategic Coordination*

cial success seems to lie in the ingenious system of limits and institutional compromises that are built into it so as to ensure its compatibility with the flourishing of the rest of the society. These limits include public debate on policy formation, parliamentary veto power over policy, and implementational efficiency through competition rather than micromanagement. Also, by way of limits, planners leave half or more of the economy outside strategic political influences entirely and refrain from any abridgement of the vitality of markets. The limitations built into this system seem to dramatically increase both its public support and its operational effect.

Objectives and Results

We have examined the dynamic of policymaking for Japan's strategic economy at the highest levels, and we have also looked at the sophisticated means by which abstract economic goals are articulated and implemented in the real economy. Let us consider now the kinds of things Japanese statesmen seem to have been pursuing in the strategic economic system and the kinds of results they have achieved.

(Note that there are almost no women among the career professional employees of the supervising economic ministries or of Japanese corporations. Japanese traditions in this particular, as in many others, are very different from our own.)

Predictability: Multilevel Planning and Low-Risk Investment

Improved predictability is one consequence of planning. MITI makes five-year plans and implements them through industrial associations, cartels, and the like. This means that MITI has a good idea of what will happen in the economy for five years, and it means that everyone else also does. Will automaking double? Will computer production double? Will the demand for silicon chips double? The answers are present in MITI's plans. Everyone in a position of authority in the economy more or less knows what the future holds. This makes it easier to prepare for it.[24]

Once MITI publishes its plans, industries at all levels as well as local governments use them to develop their own plans, much as subordinate military staffs orient their plans to those of higher headquarters.[25] Commercial market systems do not have deliberate multilevel planning to achieve strategic goals, except at corporate level and below. Nationally coordinated multilevel planning is a common feature, however, of modern military systems. A given nation's general staff develops plans that assign a mission to each theater. Theater staffs develop plans to implement their portion, assigning a part of the mission to each of their corps, and so on downward. Lower-echelon staffs plan their own operations because they know their assets and their mission better than the national headquarters staff does. It is fairly easy for the lower-echelon staffs to plan once they know what the overall goal is, what their particular mission is, and what the units next to them are doing.

Modern combined-arms warfare requires many combat elements to be brought to bear at once in a complex orchestration. An overarching plan at the top, with autonomously developed but compatible plans at each level below, makes this possible. Rapid industrial growth requires many production factors to be brought simultaneously to bear: funds, materials, skilled labor, new technology, producers' durables, transport facilities, new markets, political troubleshooting, and so on. Consistent success at synchronizing all this is possible because of the one plan that begets many plans: multilevel planning. It is essentially the same device long used by modern armies to move their millions.

Indeed, MITI does far more than improve predictability and provide plans: It largely eliminates investment risk. MITI guarantees steady growth and continuously brisk economic activity. It apportions expansion of capacity among producers, apportions markets, offers low-cost insurance against export losses, and allows tax-free cash reserves against domestic losses.[26] We shall see in examining the Japanese banking system that MITI and MOF offer low-interest, tax-exempt capital, capital that is almost free. At the same time MITI provides a wide range of other conditions favorable to growth. Japanese enterprises are highly leveraged and commonly assume development debt equal to 70 percent of their assets and more. Japanese business leaders seem unconcerned about risk. But in fact there may be relatively little risk. MITI takes steps to reduce the risk at each step of the way.[27]

The Record

Japan's postwar economic performance is commonly characterized by observers as being simply miraculous. Between 1952 and 1985, Japan's GDP grew from 13.8 trillion yen to 291.8 trillion yen, an increase of 21-fold in nominal terms. In real terms, according to the government's official *Japan Statistical Yearbook*, Japan's economy was more than six times as large in 1973 as it had been in 1952. These decades, 1952–1973, are referred to by economists as "the years of rapid growth." The unparalleled expansion of these two decades was achieved by means of an annual growth rate that averaged 9 percent. Rapid growth of GDP has been one of the characteristics of Japan's postwar economy. Overall growth is also at times explicitly stated by MITI as being one of the goals of its economic policies, in its National Income Doubling Plan of 1960, for example.[28]

Full employment is another characteristic of the postwar economy. Between 1953 and 1987, Japanese unemployment ranged between 1.1 percent and 2.8 percent. These rates are among the lowest in the industrialized world. During this same period, wages have risen astronomically. Manufacturing wages in 1985 were 22.2 times what they were in 1952, in real terms. The average worker made 22 times as much for each hour worked. Full employment and improvement of living standards are also often cited by MITI as policy objectives when announcing five-year plans.[29]

It should be noted, however, that GDP growth is not distributed evenly by sector. The lion's share of it is in manufacturing. Real GDP grew by over 6 times from 1952 to 1973; manufacturing in real terms grew by nearly 15 times, on average more than twice as fast as GDP. Moreover, the manufacturing growth rate is not distributed evenly among industries. Annual growth rates for manufacturing as a whole in the years 1952 to 1973 range from -2 percent to 25 percent and usually fall between 7 and 20 percent, average annual growth being 13 percent. For strategic industries, however, those designated as priority industries by MITI, growth rates are commonly 30 to 50 percent per year (see Figure 1.4), and sometimes more.[30]

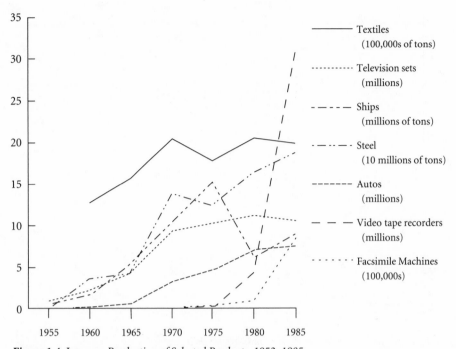

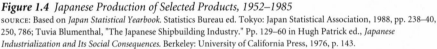

Figure 1.4 *Japanese Production of Selected Products, 1952–1985*
SOURCE: Based on *Japan Statistical Yearbook*. Statistics Bureau ed. Tokyo: Japan Statistical Association, 1988, pp. 238–40, 250, 786; Tuvia Blumenthal, "The Japanese Shipbuilding Industry." Pp. 129–60 in Hugh Patrick ed., *Japanese Industrialization and Its Social Consequences*. Berkeley: University of California Press, 1976, p. 143.

Very Rapid Growth

There appears to be no broadly based groundswell in the economy but rather very rapid increase in certain industries. MITI develops a chosen industry to the point of self-sustaining preeminence, then moves on to develop another. A priority industry characteristically has a 5- or 10-year period of very rapid growth, sometimes as high as 50 to 100 percent per year, followed by a more level period of gradual growth, stability, or even decline (see Figure 1.5).

In a typical year during the so-called rapid-growth period, Japan's GDP grew 9 percent, its manufacturing sector grew 13 percent, and favored strategic industries grew 30–50 percent. This growth is sometimes attributed to some intangible quality of Japanese culture or of the economic environment.[31] In fact, however, almost all of the growth seems to have been in priority industries, when and to the degree specified in MITI's plans, and as long as they were nourished by nearly free capital from the BOJ. Production growth in any sector, say, consumer electronics, all seems to have taken place in a dozen firms who had direct phone lines to MITI.

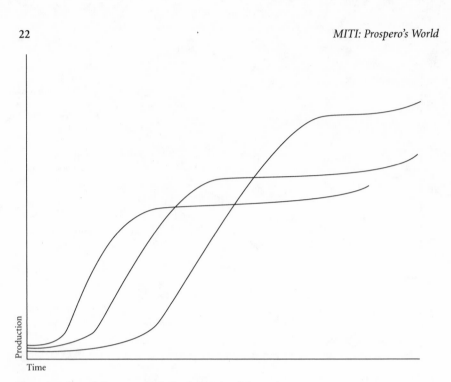

Figure 1.5 Growth Pattern of Priority Industries, Schematic

There was other robust economic activity, but it seems to have been derivative. In other words, the general prosperity seems to have been driven by the lucrative policy activity, not vice versa.

Value Added

MITI appears to develop industries in a careful sequence, and its criterion for sequencing seems at least in part to be a strategic one. Which new industry, if launched, would give Japan the greatest strategic benefits given Japan's real resources? What industry is within reach, will provide leverage in world markets, will provide products prized by Japanese consumers, will provide higher wages for Japanese employees, and will keep the road open for further industrial development later? In practice, Japan from 1945 to 1985 moved from light industries (textiles and toys) to heavy industries (steel, ships, autos) to fine industries (electronics and optics) to information industries (computers, robotics).

Observers of MITI, and of course MITI itself, describe this developmental sequencing as simply a shift up to higher and higher levels of "value added." Newly chosen industries characteristically require more advanced technology, more capital investment, and a more technologically skilled work force, than do their predecessors. They also tend to yield an advantageous global market position and higher wages at home.[32]

Inducing Kondratieff Cycles

Christopher Freeman in his skillful analysis of Japanese technology policy has noted that Japanese planners think not only in terms of developing a particular industry over 5 or 10 years but also in terms of developing compatible families of industries, anticipating much longer developmental periods. They coordinate the rise of whole new families of industries. In other words, planners work in terms of larger "techno-economic paradigms." They not only shift up from one industry to another. They may also deliberately shift the whole economy (and concomitantly the whole society) from one qualitative level to another.[33]

Earlier long transformational cycles, first described by Nikolai Kondratieff, began in the 1780s and were based on textiles (1780s), railways (1830s), electricity (1880s), and autos (1930s). Each wave, according to Kondratieff, depended on a new set of technological breakthroughs and on some newly abundant and inexpensive factor input: cotton, coal, or steel. Each wave lasted 50 or so years and left the industrial environment fundamentally transformed. Freeman suggests that Japanese economic leaders in the 1980s fashioned a fifth wave, an "information and communication technology paradigm" based on new computer technology and relying on silicon chips as its abundant new factor input. This paradigm encompasses production of computers, telecommunications equipment, robotics, numerically controlled tools, intelligent automated production equipment, and the like, which in their ensemble may transform the quality both of the industrial environment and of society at large.[34]

MITI's Objectives

Whether or not MITI can deliberately induce qualitative changes in industry comparable to the original industrial revolution, it is obvious that Japanese planners may be as resourceful in their purposes as they are in the means they employ. Planning objectives include the obvious ones: rapid growth without intermission, full employment, ever-rising wages. But MITI may also entertain goals that are more fundamental: qualitative amelioration of the whole industrial and social environment, limned out decades in advance.

*   *   *

We have now briefly explored Prospero's universe: how economic policy is made in Japan, the dynamics and structures that accommodate implementation, and the kinds of domestic objectives toward which all this extraordinary activity is aimed. Economic policy formation and implementation in Japan have certain features in common with strategic systems in the West, namely military systems and diplomatic systems. Japanese economic phenomena in the favored techno-industrial sectors are in some respects unlike the market arrangements of Western economies. Strategic organization has given Japan uniquely advantageous results in the domestic economy, including doubling of the GDP every few years, sustained prosperity, constant upgrading of the techno-industrial base, brisk wage growth, and the near disappearance of poverty in the nation. The previous brief inquiry will enable us now to look more closely at the structure of MITI and the mediating institutions that are its usual minions.

Notes

1. For policy being bureaucratically made, see, for example, Chalmers Johnson, "Japan: Who Governs?" *Journal of Japanese Studies* 2.1 (Aut 75): 1–28, pp. 10–11.

2. On the Industrial Structure Council, see Chalmers Johnson, *MITI and the Japanese Miracle* (Stanford, CA: Stanford University Press, 1982), pp. 47–48; Clyde V. Prestowitz, *Trading Places* (New York: Basic Books, 1988), pp. 129–30.

3. Haruhiro Fukui, "Economic Planning in Postwar Japan," *Asian Survey* 12.4 (Apr 72): 327–48, p. 338.

4. Prestowitz, p. 130.

5. Cf. Karel Van Wolferen, *The Enigma of Japanese Power* (New York: Alfred A. Knopf, 1989).

6. See, for example, Johnson, "Who Governs?" pp. 10–11.

7. Chalmers Johnson, "MITI, MPT, and the Telecom Wars," pp. 177–240 in Chalmers Johnson, Laura D'Andrea Tyson, and John Zysman eds., *Politics and Productivity* (New York: Ballinger, 1989), pp. 179, 198–99; Prestowitz, pp. 117–19.

8. Johnson, "MITI, MPT," pp. 198, 199–200; Ira C. Magaziner and Thomas M. Hout, *Japanese Industrial Policy* (Berkeley, CA: Institute of International Studies, 1980), p. 36; Prestowitz, pp. 118–19.

9. See, for example, Prestowitz, p. 144.

10. Compare Johnson, *MITI and the Japanese Miracle*, p. 316. Johnson likens the Diet-MITI relationship in economic policymaking to "the American legislative branch's relationship to the wartime Manhattan Project or to the postwar nuclear submarine development program."

11. Cf. Chalmers Johnson, *Japan's Public Policy Companies* (Washington, DC: American Enterprise Institute, 1978), p. 23. Johnson has noted the similarity of MITI's influence to that of the U.S. Defense Department.

12. See Michael Gerlach, "*Keiretsu* Organization in the Japanese Economy," pp. 141–74 in C. Johnson, L. Tyson, and J. Zysman, *Politics and Productivity*, pp. 146–49.

13. For a developed perspective on Japanese industrial associations, see Leonard Lynn and Timothy J. McKeown, *Organizing Business: Trade Associations in America and Japan* (Washington, DC: American Enterprise Institute, 1988).

14. On cartels, see Eleanor M. Hadley, *Antitrust in Japan* (Princeton: Princeton University Press, 1970), pp. 357–89.

15. Ezra F. Vogel, *Japan as Number One* (New York: Harper and Row, 1979), p. 72.

16. See T. J. Pempel, "Japanese Foreign Economic Policy: The Domestic Bases for International Behavior," pp. 723–74 in Peter J. Katzenstein ed., *Between Power and Plenty: Foreign Economic Policies of Advanced Industrial Countries*, published as a special edition of *International Organization* 31.4 (Aut 77): 581–920 (whole volume), p. 734.

17. For the 11 million figure, see Charles J. McMillan, *The Japanese Industrial System* (Berlin: Walter de Gruyter, 1984), p. 59. For the 1.7 million figure, see Gerlach, "*Keiretsu* Organization," p. 145.

18. Ibid., pp. 58–59.

19. See *Tsusan handobukku* [*MITI Handbook*], Tsusan handobukku henshu iinkai ed. [MITI Handbook Editing Committee ed.] (Tokyo: Shokokaikan, 1989) [hereafter *MITI Handbook*], pp. 203–14, 528–29; *Tsusho sangyo roppo* [*International Trade and Industry Laws*], Tsusho sangyo-sho ed. [MITI ed.] (Tokyo: Marui Kobunsha, 1988) [hereafter *MITI Laws*], pp. 1359–1560. Both the *MITI Handbook* and *MITI Laws* are publications compiled by MITI and distributed to the general public through Japanese government bookstores.

20. Yasukichi Yasuba, "The Evolution of Dualistic Wage Structure," pp. 249–98 in Hugh Patrick ed., *Japanese Industrialization and Its Social Consequences* (Berkeley: University of California Press, 1976), p. 249.

21. For further discussion of the banking system, see the section of Chapter 3 entitled "Control of Capital Flow: Strategic Investment," and following.

22. For further discussion of PPCs, see the section of Chapter 3 entitled "Control of Materials Flow: Public Policy Companies," and following.

23. Johnson, *MITI and the Japanese Miracle*, pp. 315, 317, 318.

24. On this point see also Joseph A. Schumpeter, *Capitalism, Socialism and Democracy* (New York: Harper and Row, 1975 [1942]), p. 186.

25. McMillan, p. 71. For a list of the regional development plans that have accompanied national development plans, see Kiyoji Murata and Isamu Ota eds., *An Industrial Geography of Japan* (London: Bell and Hyman, 1980), pp. 180–81.

26. For capacity apportionment, see John Zysman, *Governments, Markets, and Growth* (Ithaca, NY: Cornell University Press, 1983), pp. 242–43.

27. This condition is described by Prestowitz, p. 131.

28. *Japan Statistical Yearbook* [hereafter *Japan Statistics*], Statistics Bureau ed. (Tokyo: Japan Statistical Association, 1988), p. 790; Fukui, p. 338. Note that *Japan Statistics* is the official statistical yearbook series issued by the Japanese government. The *Japanese Statistics* series changes its constant yen base at 1965, so the calculation of GDP expansion in this paragraph assumes that GDP growth for 1965 approximated the average rate for the 1952–1973 period of 9.2 percent.

29. *Japan Statistics*, p. 785; Fukui, p. 338.

30. See, for example, *Japan Statistics*, pp. 238–39, 250, 785–86. See also Prestowitz, p. 167.

31. In this regard cf. for example Ryoshin Minami, *The Economic Development of Japan* (London: Macmillan Press, 1986).

32. See, for example, Michael Borrus, James Millstein, and John Zysman, *U.S.-Japanese*

Competition in the Semiconductor Industry (Berkeley, CA: Institute of International Relations, 1982), pp. 47–48. See also Magaziner and Hout, p. 9.

33. See Christopher Freeman, *Technology Policy and Economic Performance: Lessons from Japan* (London: Pinter, 1987), pp. 64–79, and Nikolai D. Kondratieff, *The Long Wave Cycle* (New York: Richardson and Snyder, 1984 [1925]).

34. Freeman, pp. 66–71.

2
Neo-Zaibatsu and Cartels: Coordination and Competition

Strategic planning of industrial growth would appear to be impractical, "a task of unmanageable complication," as Schumpeter put it. Unless one knows how it is done, it seems impossible. The basic device that makes strategic economy possible (and plausible) is essentially the same device, of relatively recent origin, that makes the coordinated movement of modern armies possible: mediating levels of implementation. These are permanent staff structures that lie between operational corporations and the national political authority. They have their own unique characteristics, objectives, and dynamics. They have a mission and a genius that make them fundamentally different both from the political authority above and from operational units below.

In 1789, field armies in Europe were small and had only one permanent formation: the regiment. Between 1789 and 1804, the new French republic, to marshal unprecedented scores of thousands of troops, added more and more layers of command: brigades, divisions, corps, and armies. These were permanent formations with their own staffs, and with all arms. They allowed Napoleon to do something new: With them he could move 60,000 men with a few simple orders, not in lock step but doing different and complex things in elaborate orchestration, much of it at the discretion of lower commanders and even individual soldiers. This was possible because Napoleon's simple orders were interpreted and articulated, translated into many particular operations, by many levels of talented staffs between Napoleon and the troops. Moving armies in this way had been unthinkable a generation before. It was possible for Napoleon because of the "invention" of middle levels of command. The new strategic organization, and the vast resources France poured into it, allowed Napoleon for a time to sweep all before him. Within a few years, of course, other services adopted these innovative methods and could meet Napoleon as equals in the field.

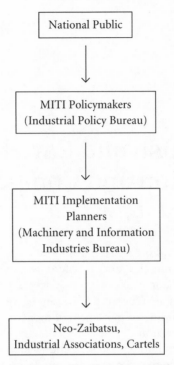

Figure 2.1 *Pattern of Industrial Coordination Illustrating MITI's Two Functional Levels,
Schematic*

Japanese planners have in effect established analogous institutions in their industrial economy: permanent formations at successively higher levels than the corporation that converge on the central policy planners of the state. This makes it possible for a MITI bureau chief to provide a simple policy objective—doubling steel production, for example—and tens of thousands of people begin to toil in complex ways, using usually their own best judgement to make this happen. Without several layers of staffs to coordinate and orchestrate and match real resources to the abstract objectives, strategic planning for industry would be hard to imagine.

Much of the unique genius of the Japanese economy lies in a whole category of mediating institutions that does not exist in the U.S. economy. It is perhaps in these arrangements above all that Japan's economy is truly original. U.S. political scientists study the Japanese government; U.S. business professors study Japanese corporations; U.S. economists study the Japanese market. All these entities have a U.S. counterpart. Much of the work of Japan's strategic economy is done, however, in a zone of integrative institutions that does not exist at all in the U.S. economy. Most U.S. scholars, with little sense of their nature or purpose, are not attracted to the study of these institutions. Yet without them there would have been no economic miracle in Japan. Even Schumpeter, who in his *Capitalism, Socialism and Democracy* seems to anticipate several features of today's Japanese system, barely mentions the complex structures that successful strategic planning requires between government and corporations. A future economy, Schumpeter wrote, must "set up an authority for each industry that is to manage it and cooperate with the central board which controls and coordinates all these ... managing boards."[1] But, alas, Schumpeter did not elaborate.

The advantages of multilevel staffing for strategic coordination are known to business school professors. Alfred Chandler in his *Strategy and Structure* describes the decisive competitive value of multilevel, multidivisional organizational structure for corporations.[2] Charles McMillan, James Abegglen, and others have suggested that MITI operates the whole Japanese economy in much the same way that an Anglo-American corporation manages its own "portfolio."[3] There is much truth to this, but it is also true that coordinating 30 corporations is a qualitatively different activity in some respects from running one corporation and that overseeing a whole national economy is different again. For the notion of permanent staff structures that lie between operational units and the national political authority and that have their own proper characteristics, objectives, and dynamics, Anglo-American readers are well-advised to look to the strategic literature, that is, literature on national military security, where such notions are maturely developed and, of course, routine.

In the pages that follow I will attempt concisely to explore the world of the great mediating institutions in the Japanese system: how they are supervised, created, and maintained; their relationship to the government, to each other, and to their corporate members; and what each, broadly speaking, is supposed to achieve. We have already seen that MITI instructs and coordinates the Japanese economy through three categories of institution: neo-zaibatsu, industrial associations, and cartels. Let us examine the role of each of these, beginning with MITI itself.

MITI: The Great Translator

MITI appears in Western literature variously as powerful, professional, magnificently efficient, or even ominous. It is usually seen, however, as being monolithic, a unitary entity. In reality, MITI is a complex and lively affair, and that liveliness is a key to its success. MITI may be thought of as having a top and a bottom. At the top it surveys its public constituencies and the world and sets industrial policy objectives. At the bottom MITI metes these objectives out to the great industrial organizations that are best able to implement them. Broadly speaking, MITI has two distinct functions: (1) making policy and (2) converting policy into con-

Table 2.1   *Internal Bureaus of MITI Grouped by Function*

GENERAL ADMINISTRATION
AND POLICY
Minister's Secretariat

TRADE POLICY	DOMESTIC POLICY
International Trade Policy Bureau	Industrial Policy Bureau
TRADE IMPLEMENTATION	DOMESTIC IMPLEMENTATION
International Trade Administration Bureau	Machine and Information Industries Bureau (MIIB) (High-Tech Industries) Basic Industries Bureau (Heavy Industries) Consumer Goods Industries Bureau (Light Industries) Industrial Location and Environmental Protection Bureau

SOURCE: Derived from *Tsusan handobukku [MITI Handbook]*. MITI Handbook Editing Committee ed. Tokyo: Shokokaikan, 1989, pp. i–ii, pp. 3–120 passim.

crete plans and starting these down the coordinative chain toward the institutional zones where they will be implemented (see Figure 2.1). These several functions are apparent from casual scrutiny of MITI's internal structure: Three of its major agencies ("internal bureaus") address policy formation, and five address implementation (see Table 2.1).

Policy implementation functions are handled by the industries bureaus, and cutting-edge growth is handled by the Machine and Information Industries Bureau (MIIB). The whole raison d'être of this bureau is to translate policy objectives into usable instructions for the industrial associations and neo-zaibatsu and, of course, to monitor compliance. Even Prospero must instruct Ariel and chastise Caliban. (We will not dwell here on coordinative discipline, "chastising Caliban." For a few cases of MITI sanctions, though, see, for example, Magaziner and Hout 1980, pp. 60–61, regarding overproduction by Sumitomo Metals in 1965, and Lynn and McKeown 1988, p. 93, regarding overproduction by Nisshin Spinning of cotton goods in 1966 and by Idemitsu Kosan of petroleum in the same year.) The distinctive mission and genius of the middle levels of coordination of the Japanese economy are present at the highest levels in the implementational bureaus of MITI itself. The structure of the premier strategic industries bureau, MIIB, reflects this mission of translating policy into plans for particular industries. MIIB is a microcosm of the whole machine industries environment. Every machine-manufacturing industry of strategic importance is represented (see Table 2.2).

Table 2.2 *Divisions of MITI's Machinery and Information Industries Bureau (MIIB)*

General Affairs

Aircraft and Ordnance
Automobile
Cast and Wrought Products
Electrical Machinery and Consumer Electronics
Electronics Policy
Industrial Electronics
Industrial Machinery
Information, Computer and Communications Policy Office
Information Services
Information Systems Development
Space Industry
Vehicle

SOURCE: *Tsusan handobukku [MITI Handbook]*. MITI Handbooking Editing Committee ed. Tokyo: Shokokaikan, 1989, pp. 98–110.

MIIB's divisions, inevitably, have jurisdiction also over the relevant families of industrial associations, which, of course, is the reason MIIB exists and is structured as it is. There are hundreds of organizations, many of them industrial associations, under MIIB. MIIB's Automobile Division, for example, watches over the Japan Automobile Manufacturers Association and 11 other auto-production-related associations (see Table 2.3). This means that when policy for the auto industry changes, meaning usually a production increase, there are knowledgeable specialized staffs both at the level of MIIB's Automobile Division and at the next lower level of the Japan Automobile Manufacturers Association to translate the policy goals into feasible mandates for particular corporations.

MITI: The Great Reconstructer

Even so, performance at the corporation level, once the mandate is communicated, is guaranteed by competition, not by government interference. The government provides capital and materials, and the other production factors it coordinates, to the relevant strategic corporations. Those that perform best at increasing capacity, raising quality, and lowering costs are rewarded with more access to capital and materials the following year, giving them a decisive advantage over their rivals. A corporation that wishes to stay on MITI's list dare not fall too far behind.

Basically, MITI draws upon other sectors of the society to provide strategic corporations with resources for expansion. The strategic managers and workers involved at the receiving end of this providence do not experience it as coercion so much as an environment of opportunity where energetic action will be richly rewarded. Strategic corporation managers almost always respond to this with alac-

Table 2.3 *Automotive Industrial Associations Affiliated with MIIB*

Japan Automobile Manufacturers Association, Inc.

Japan Auto Accessories Manufacturers Association
Japan Auto-Body Industries Association, Inc.
Japan Automobile Research Institute
Japan Automotive Machinery and Tool Manfacturers Association
Japan Automotive Service Equipment Association
Japan Automotive Products Association
Japan Auto Parts Industries Association
Japan Electrical Vehicle Association
Japan Mini-Vehicles Association
Japan Motor Industrial Federation
Society of Automotive Engineers of Japan, Inc.

SOURCE: *Tsusan handobukku [MITI Handbook]*. MITI Handbook Editing Committee ed. Tokyo: Shokokaikan, 1989, pp. 847–54.

rity. We have already explored in Chapter 1 some of the advantages of this approach of setting the strategic objectives, then leaving the individual corporations completely free to pursue them.

Part of the genius of this arrangement is that it relies heavily on positive incentives. Institutions, like individuals, respond more vitally to positive reinforcement than to negative. MITI's strategic instruction to corporations, in tandem with generous capital from BOJ, work much like the U.S. government's giving out defense-related research contracts to U.S. universities. The universities know what they are supposed to do, clamor to do it, and if they succeed their lucrative grant is renewed or increased. Government thus guides the research, but recipients do not feel forced or stifled. Their experience is the exhilaration of success, not the numbness of coercion.

Much of the vitality of the Japanese system depends on competition. Corporations are motivated by a sense of rivalry with the other institutions that are their peers. They are motivated by pride, by élan. But they are also motivated by the knowledge that if their performance is wanting, precious resources may be denied to them and handed to their rivals, a process that, if repeated, might threaten their institutional survival. Receiving their external budget from government-coordinated banks depends not only on compliance but on successful compliance compared to others.

Competition brings about discipline in a noninterventionist way. MITI has other good reasons for nourishing pluralist competition, however, besides the enlivening force of rivalry. A pluralist approach, with many agencies working on the same task, means they are more likely among them to discover effective new methods. Once these "best methods" are apparent, they can be shared with all participants. Also, pluralism provides for redundancy. Should any of the key producers fail, as some inevitably do, other capable producers are available for MITI to turn to, at little cost to MITI or the economy. Moreover, there is never a situation where a single producer can dilute its performance or say no, believing it is MITI's only option. This, of course, is what competition means.

In any case, to achieve a lively spirit of rivalry, cross-fertilization of "best methods," redundancy, and freedom from single-producer intransigencies, MITI must ensure the presence in any given field of a number of capable providers. At the same time, MITI does not want too many providers because they would then lack economies of scale, small ones could not compete effectively against large ones, and numerousness of itself would make the providers difficult to coordinate.

For maximum effect, MITI wants not too few and not too many. In practice this means 6 to 10. In any given area, MITI strives to sustain 6 to 10 major corporations capable of achieving its production objectives.[4] Random events seldom provide exactly 6 to 10 major producers, but no matter. MITI vigorously intervenes in the corporate world to establish an efficient structural environment, namely 6 to 10 major producers. Ezra Vogel likens MITI to the National Football League, structuring its conferences to get just the right number of teams to ensure both brisk rivalry and quality of play.[5]

In a fledgling industry, MITI usually has too many small firms participating. MITI solves this problem by rapidly promoting promising small concerns such as Sony or Honda by feeding them business or else solves it by compulsory merging of firms, or both.[6] MITI thus moves rapidly from an environment of scores of small producers to a field of 10. New entrants are then discouraged by MITI's denying them license to import technology, for example.[7] There appears to be little movement among corporations in such a field of 6 to 10 to merge further to gain a monopoly position, probably because the field of 10 now has the force of tradition but also because such action might evoke a negative response both from MITI and the larger public.

MITI may use its informal influence to obtain mergers or exclude new entrants. MITI also, however, has legal empowerment to reconstruct whole industries where the national interest requires it. These powers are conferred on MITI under the Law for the Promotion of Enterprise Rationalization, the Special Industrial Structure Amelioration Temporary Measures Law, the Facilitation of Industrial Structure Conversion Temporary Measures Law, and their auxiliary ordinances.[8] MITI is the great reconstructer as a matter of law.

Western economists have little to say about nationwide constant, deliberate reconfiguration of institutional structure. There is again a useful military analogy, however. Modern military services devote continuous attention to changing and perfecting force structure. They routinely create or dissolve formations of millions of persons for no better reason than changes in the society's perceived needs. There are contingents of officers in every modern service that, as in MITI's Industrial Policy Bureau, do nothing but tend to constant improvement of the force structure in size, balance, and configuration, sweeping away obsolete units and fashioning new ones.[9] Deliberately changing institutional structure to achieve larger political and social purposes is routine for twentieth-century military staffs, as it is for MITI.

MITI turns strategic policy into concrete plans that the middle levels of economic organization can work from. MITI also tends to economic structure and reconstructs the corporate environment at middle levels of organization and below, as needed, to ensure efficiency of response to policy objectives.

Neo-Zaibatsu: Nonobstructive Rivalry

Perhaps the best known middle level of strategic-economic coordination in Japan is the neo-zaibatsu. There are six of these, consisting of about 30 corporations each. Their main function is to coordinate activities that require cooperation among corporations of different types, as we have seen. Almost everything MITI does, it does in part through neo-zaibatsu corporations. Each neo-zaibatsu has sufficiently varied assets that it can, if need be, meet MITI goals without drawing on resources from outside its own group.

Each neo-zaibatsu is a kind of strategic economy in miniature, a complete microcosm. Each neo-zaibatsu bank and presidents' club must do what MITI does, namely supervise complex corporate interactions to produce rapid growth. Neo-zaibatsu banks and presidents' clubs practice what might be called noncoercive supervision. A neo-zaibatsu bank exercises major de facto influence over neo-zaibatsu member corporations, but as with MITI, this is in the nature of instruction and coordination, not specific command. Also as with MITI, the degree of influence is nonetheless great because the group bank governs the member corporation's credit, which is its only major source of external funding.

Group banks are responsible for the performance of their members. When one of the members stumbles, it is the group bank that steps in and takes over management and restructuring until the company is again sound. This is possible because bank officials, like the staff of MITI's MIIB, are career-specialized by industry. In the mid-1970s when the Mazda Corporation (Toyo Kogyo) nearly went bankrupt, its group bank, Sumitomo, placed eight bank officials in key Mazda posts. They exercised direction over the company until it became viable again in the early 1980s. When in the mid-1980s Akai Electric, a tape-deck manufacturer, neared bankruptcy, its group bank, Mitsubishi, sent in three officials who directed the company back to solvency.[10] In all this the group bank does for its own neo-zaibatsu essentially what MIIB does for the larger industrial environment. It is the responsible coordinating staff.

Nonobstructive, or nonconflictive, rivalry characterizes relations among neo-zaibatsu. The neo-zaibatsu exists to maximize cooperation among its 30 corporate members. Each neo-zaibatsu competes, however, with the other neo-zaibatsu. In other words, the neo-zaibatsu compete at cooperation for rapid growth. Neo-zaibatsu compete to implement all of MITI's objectives—expanding capacity, raising quality, and lowering costs. They do not, however, compete at obstructing each other in these missions. They compete at execution but do not compete at denying each other resources, whether funds, materials, or technology. They do not usually compete on price to the user. If a neo-zaibatsu does well in realizing the public's economic objectives, it is rewarded by MITI and the public with funds, responsibility, and prestige. A neo-zaibatsu would forfeit its right to this kind of recognition if it impaired the public interest by obstructing other public servants in their mission. All neo-zaibatsu competitive energies are thus focused on production, and none on preventing production by others. Neo-zaibatsu practice creative competition, not obstructive competition.[11]

The analogy to theater command again works here. Ambitious theater commanders compete for resources, responsibility, and public reputation. They do this by outdoing each other in achieving mission objectives. But they never attack each other's forces or destroy each other's supplies. Doing so would bring the severest of sanctions from the commander in chief and the public. Antisocial conduct against their peers would end their ambitions. Japanese neo-zaibatsu and neo-zaibatsu corporations, like Marine divisions, compete, but at engaging the mission, never each other. That is what strategic organization means.

Nonobstructive patterns of rivalry are expected and required among neo-zaibatsu in their relations with each other. They share the same larger goal, after all: growth of the economic system of which they are a part.

Neo-Zaibatsu: Structure

There are six neo-zaibatsu of about 30 corporations each. Four of them—Mitsubishi, Mitsui, Sumitomo, and Fuyo (formerly Yasuda)—are continuations of the big four zaibatsu of the prewar period.[12] The other two, Sanwa and Daiichi, were organized after the war, partly from elements of smaller prewar zaibatsu such as Shibusawa and Nissan. As was true of the prewar four, these six groups' 180 members hold about 25 percent of all assets in the Japanese economy.[13]

Among the six neo-zaibatsu, there are some 180 member corporations. As of 1982, Mitsubishi had 28; Mitsui, 24; Sumitomo, 21; Fuyo, 29; Sanwa, 40; and Daiichi, 45, for an exact total of 187 corporations. Each of these 187 corporations has in turn 11 to 200 client companies subordinated to it, for a total, as of 1974, of 8,476 companies. The average is 45 affiliated client companies per neo-zaibatsu member. These 187 neo-zaibatsu member corporations and their 8,476 client companies, plus a few hundred companies like Matsushita and its group that make and export consumer goods so lucratively that they are not so reliant on neo-zaibatsu banks, represent the whole structure of the strategic economy. In this sense they also mark the limits of the strategic economy. In terms of numbers of companies, this configuration represents only a small percentage of the 1.7 million incorporated firms in Japan.[14]

Since each neo-zaibatsu is a self-sufficient cooperative group, each must have member corporations in every major industrial category. The Mitsubishi group, for example, encompasses industries in finance, international trade, construction, real estate, textiles, chemicals, oil, glass and cement, paper, steel, aluminum, heavy machinery, electrical and optical, shipping, warehousing, and other areas. Corporate members include, among others, Mitsubishi Bank, Mitsubishi Corporation (trade), Mitsubishi Construction, Mitsubishi Chemical, Asahi Glass, Mitsubishi Mining, Mitsubishi Steel, Mitsubishi Aluminum, Mitsubishi Heavy Industries, Mitsubishi Motors, Mitsubishi Electric, Nippon Kogaku (Nikon), Nippon Yusen Kaisha (N.Y.K., shipping), and Kirin Beer. Thus if the Nikon Corporation wishes to double camera production, it can quickly find reliable financing, glass and metal supplies, and global market outlets and carry out plant construction and overseas shipping without going outside the Mitsubishi group. Dealing with stable allies in all these areas expedites cooperation and reduces risk. The five other neo-zaibatsu have a similar array of members in these same industrial categories, with the same object.[15]

It is worth noting that Mitsubishi has four financial members: Mitsubishi Bank, Mitsubishi Trust, Meiji Life Insurance, and Tokio (sic) Fire and Marine Insurance. Mitsubishi Bank is one of the 12 city banks, which are conduits of funds from BOJ to strategic industry. Each neo-zaibatsu has this same approximate configuration of financial institutions: a main bank, a trust bank, a life insurance company, and a casualty insurance company. Neo-zaibatsu insurance companies hold over 50 percent of Japan's total insurance capital. Insurance companies, like the 12 city banks, are a means of channeling funds from the society at large to strategic industries.[16]

Neo-zaibatsu membership is usually defined by participation in a given neo-zaibatsu presidents' club. Presidents of the member firms gather for a meeting once a month to socialize and coordinate their activities. For Mitsubishi it is the Friday Club, for Mitsui the Second Thursday Club, and so on. There is a chairmanship that rotates monthly. Although membership lists are published, the clubs have no legally binding control over the members.[17]

The neo-zaibatsu are also linked by mutual ties of equity, credit, and commerce. They own each other's stock, borrow each other's capital, and buy each other's goods.[18] This means they normally deal with known and well-disposed partners in most of their activities, which expedites affairs considerably. They have a stake in each other's success and so need not waste time and energy in a struggle to extract profit from each other. Their struggle is against other groups, not against other corporations in their own. This, of course, is the principle of nonconflictive rivalry at work within neo-zaibatsu.

Neo-zaibatsu members do a disproportionate share of their borrowing, about 20 percent, from banks and insurance companies in their own group. Lending by the neo-zaibatsu bank represents a kind of endorsement, however, an indispensable imprimatur that allows members to borrow smaller amounts from numerous outside banks. The neo-zaibatsu's main bank is the primus inter pares of the group, and the bank, not the presidents' club, serves as the mini-MITI, cum mini-BOJ, that oversees the neo-zaibatsu's activities.[19]

Neo-zaibatsu are responsive to the public purpose in part because they are largely a self-owned constellation of firms in which there is relatively little participation by genuinely external private holders. The basic pattern is this: Each of the 30 member companies owns 2 or so percent of the stock of each of the others. Thus about 60 percent of each member's stock, a dominant controlling interest, is stably held by other members. The other 40 percent of the stock is freely traded on the stock market, but even most of that is stably held in small amounts by companies belonging to other neo-zaibatsu. Private holders can purchase small amounts of neo-zaibatsu stock, but under prevailing conditions it is extremely difficult for them to approach a controlling interest. In practice, larger member companies—insurance, banking, manufacturing—tend to hold somewhat more than 2 percent of their fellow-companies' stock; smaller member companies tend to hold somewhat less than 2 percent.[20]

More than half of all neo-zaibatsu stockholding is bilaterally mutual and offsetting. Mitsubishi Widgets and Mitsubishi Skyhooks own corresponding shares of each other's stock, quite as if they had merely exchanged stock. For the Mitsubishi group, bilateral offsetting holdings amount to 56 percent of all of the members' stock. For Mitsui it is 57 percent and for Sumitomo it is 68 percent. One consequence of this pattern is that few dividends are ever paid into hands outside the neo-zaibatsu. That is, few dividends leave the larger galaxy of the neo-zaibatsu because neo-zaibatsu corporations pay few dividends, except to each other. There is little net movement of wealth.[21]

The 187 neo-zaibatsu corporations are not privately owned in the usual sense of being held principally by external stockholders. In functional terms, the conduct of these great flagships of strategic economy may perhaps be easier to comprehend if they are conceptualized as being more in the nature of public institutions, responsible to their peers, the public, and the government. They are interowned, which amounts, though, to being collectively self-owned. This raises interesting questions of how corporation policy can be made if there are no actively participating external owners and why the neo-zaibatsu maintain the appearance of being owned by private stockholders when functionally speaking that is not exactly the case. There are several plausible reasons for this complicated approach, which will be explored in the section of Chapter 4 entitled "The Purposes of Stock Crossholding." Suffice it here to say that crossholding creates a motivationally advantageous environment of responsibility and accountability within the member corporations and that maintaining the forms of private stockholding makes it easier to ward off attempts at micromanagement by the government.

Industrial Associations

Many of MITI's developmental objectives are implemented through the so-called industrial associations. These associations gather together all the firms in one industry. They are systematically homogeneous by industry, unlike the neo-zaibatsu, which deliberately intermix industries. Each industrial bureau of MITI has many families of industrial associations arrayed under it. Under MIIB's Electrical Machinery and Consumer Electronics Division, for example, which includes optical products, are the Japan Optical Industry Association, the Japan Telescope Manufacturers Association, the Japan Camera Industry Association, the Japan Photographic Equipment Association, the Japan Binocular Manufacturers Association, the Japan Motion Picture Equipment Industrial Association, and the Japan Microscope Manufacturers Association.[22]

Every division of every MITI industrial bureau has several families of industrial associations closely affiliated with it.[23] The industrial associations are no more and no less than the next level of implementation, just below the MITI bureaus and interacting closely with them. MITI orchestrates the economy in part through a comprehensive array of industrial associations.[24] Apparently members of an industrial association meet each year to develop proposals for their industry for the subsequent year, and a MITI official sits ex officio at these meetings. MITI takes these proposals into account when forming policy. Official policies for the industry are developed by MITI's Industrial Structure Council and Industrial Policy Bureau and eventually come back down to the industrial association.[25]

The advantage of working through industrial associations instead of individual industries is that the associations "focus interests" in a given industry so that the industry can speak with one voice. The MITI division involved need deal through only one forum, making its business dramatically simpler. The same is true of policy implementation. MITI need only present the policy to this one forum, not to every corporation separately.[26]

There are several activities in which it is especially advantageous for MITI to communicate with and influence all the members of an industry at once. These include fostering quality control methods, proliferating new technologies, setting up cooperative research arrangements to develop new technologies, and coordinating prices of materials and finished products. It is probably safe to assume that MITI conducts all these activities continually in the context of the industrial associations.

There are other compelling reasons, besides routine simplification of coordination, for MITI's working through industrial associations. Corporations in the same industry, like neo-zaibatsu, are expected to practice nonconflictive rivalry. They are supposed to compete in executing the policy but to refrain from obstructing their peers who are also in the act of implementing. Growth helps the country; asset pilferage among firms does not. In fact, close coordination is needed if corporations in the same field are to maximize their achievement without infringing on each other's performance or well-being. MITI provides this coordination or, rather, oversees the industrial association that is supposed to provide such coordination for itself. These areas include, among others, production levels, price levels, inventory levels, and materials allocation. If, for example, one steel producer cornered all the ore and another all the coking coal, both could be ruined. If all of them doubled capacity at a time of stagnant world demand, all could be ruined. If one producer used savings to double capacity while the others used theirs to cut prices, only the one who made the investment would be ruined.

To avoid all misadventures of these sorts (concerns about which may inhibit investment) and to ensure that all producers operate at maximum efficiency, policies on production levels, price levels, inventory levels, and materials allocation levels are apparently coordinated on an ongoing basis. All of a corporation staff's attention, all its competitive striving, can thus be focused on one mission: expansion and perfection of production. Everything else, to the extent possible, is coordinated and arranged. Corporations can in this way avoid the distraction of the constant, wearying endeavor to outguess and outmaneuver each other in raids on each other's resources. The corporation's best minds are thus freed to concentrate on production problems.

The industrial association functions somewhat analogously to a council of division commanders on the eve of battle. Division commanders must decide who will take what roads forward, who will receive what supplies, who will attack the enemy where. If the commanders do not arrange this, their divisions will foul each other on the roads, struggle over ill-divided supplies, or even attack each other's forces accidentally. Modern divisions are aggressive, but only against the enemy. They compete with other friendly divisions to implement the mission, not to obstruct others in doing so. Coordination with friendly units, especially the most competitive ones, greatly reduces the uncertainty and accidents that are otherwise a major hazard of their business. Nonconflictive rivalry is universally required by modern nations of their military forces. The military analogy helps shed light on why strategic industrial corporations, even aggressive, self-sufficient corporations, must toil at cooperation at all times. It helps clarify what they cooperate at and what they compete at. It helps overcome what might otherwise seem an elusive paradox. Nonobstructive rivalry is taken for granted in Anglo-American strategic thought, though Anglo-American writers in the past have not usually regarded large-scale industrial production as lying in the zone of the strategic.

MITI uses industrial associations wherever implementation requires coordination among corporations in the same field, rather than among corporations in different fields, for which MITI uses neo-zaibatsu. For efforts of industrial coordination with a more specific or short-lived purpose, MITI uses "cartels," temporary ad hoc combinations, not the ongoing, broadly based industrial associations. The industrial associations, however, do form a matrix in which cartels may be formed, and a whole industrial association may function in some respects as a cartel.[27] The dynamics of this will become more apparent when we explore the nature and purpose of cartels.

Cartels

The Japanese cartel is organized to achieve a relatively specific task for a relatively specific period of time. In this respect it is unlike the industrial associations that handle the routine and ongoing coordination activities of an industry. The cartels are analogous to an operational task force in the military. A commander, to seize a particular objective, assembles an ad hoc unit consisting of exactly the infantry, artillery, armor, and so on he believes is necessary. When the objective is taken, this specially tailored task force is disbanded.

Cartels are especially important for industries in an environment of structural change such as rapid growth or capacity reduction. Cartels are used much as industrial associations are: to develop and proliferate technology, to allocate materials and markets, and often to coordinate prices both of materials and of finished goods. These dynamics are more pronounced in an environment of change, for example, brisk increase in demand for materials in a time of growth, making coordination more necessary. Without coordination, growth capital could end up in the hands of materials brokers, not invested in new plant. Failure to coordinate prices of materials and products could easily impair the momentum for growth. Growth capital, gathered from the small sacrificial contributions of the whole population, might "leak" out of the system and be dissipated.[28]

In the U.S. tradition of industrial economy, all cooperation of private corporations to control prices, materials, production levels, and such is viewed as a harmful leveraging of a private interest against the general interest, and such activity is restricted by the U.S. Fair Trade Commission. The United States established a similar agency in Japan shortly after World War II, the Japan Fair Trade Commission (JFTC). Japanese officials, however, appear to view strategic corporations as actually being agencies of the public interest, not of the private interest, and thus regard cooperation among them for approved goals as very much representing the public interest. Certain kinds of cartel, since they represented the public interest, not the private interest, should therefore be encouraged, not restrained. Accordingly, in 1953, shortly after the U.S. occupation ended, the Japanese amended the U.S.-devised Anti-Monopoly Law to authorize certain advantageous exceptions and have been authorizing them ever since.

The JFTC thus came to have a useful function quite different from the one the Americans intended: to register the exceptions to the Anti-Monopoly Law and in effect to publicly authorize them. By this same action it de-authorizes all other cartels, that is, cartels that may serve speculator aspiration, not strategic policy. This makes it easy for government and public alike to tell which of the hundreds of existing cartels are serving a public purpose and which are not but exist instead to promote arbitrary private leverages. The JFTC performs the considerable service of preventing the latter from springing up, masquerading as the former. The evolved JFTC does yeoman service as a kind of college of heralds. An example of this was the case in July 1989 where the JFTC demanded the breakup of a cartel of beef importers consisting of the Mitsubishi, Mitsui, and C. Itoh trading companies. They had met in advance to fix the share of beef each would sell to the national beef importing monopoly, the Livestock Industry Promotion Corporation (LIPCO). The JFTC had no complaints about LIPCO, the public monopoly cartel. The JFTC intervened firmly, however, to break up the private cartel, whose offense was that it was using monopolist coercion to extract private profits from the legal public monopoly.[29]

The U.S.-inspired Anti-Monopoly Law was passed in 1947. It was amended in 1953 to allow rationalization and anti-depression cartels. Since 1953, more and more exceptions have been allowed to the Anti-Monopoly Law. More industries have been placed under the rationalization and antidepression rubrics, and new rubrics have been added. The Export and Import Law of 1953 authorized "domestic cartels of producers who are exporting" and "import cartels" addressing price and quantity of materials imported (meaning almost all materials for some industries). The Machine Industry Promotion Temporary Law of 1961 authorized rationalization cartels in machine industries for 10 years. The Electronics Industry Promotion Temporary Law of 1957 did the same for electronics industries for a seven-year term. A host of other cartels for small enterprises, mining output, and pollution control were legislated in the 1950s and 1960s.[30]

By 1973 there were 985 authorized cartels, according to the JFTC; numbers of cartels have continued to fluctuate slightly since. Eleanor Hadley has estimated that more than 28 percent of all Japanese commerce and 40 percent of export trade is cartelized. One hundred eighty "export cartels" and 10 "rationalization cartels" are apparently where much of the heavy work of coordination for strategic goals is done.[31]

It is probably a fair guess that all strategic growth industries have a cartel set up for them as soon as policymakers identify the industry. Establishment of the cartel by MITI is a routine early step in the growth process. The cartel seems sometimes to exist before the new industry does and is set up initially to coordinate the research needed before production can begin. Cartels have been established in recent decades for aircraft production, machine tools, semiconductors, and computers. Cartels' forms vary somewhat, appropriately, since their tasks vary somewhat. In machine tools, for example, the Manufacturing Share Deliberation Committee was created by the Japan Machine Tool Builders Association to determine which manufacturers would implement which kinds of machine tool production. For a cartel to grow out of the related industrial association is common, and cartels may be initiated by MITI or by the association. In this case the cartel served MITI's basic plans for machine tools that have been handed down since 1957. The machine tools cartel is a case where the form is that of a loose confederation of producing corporations.[32]

Quite different in form is the Nippon Aircraft Manufacturing Company (NAMC). NAMC is a public policy company created in 1957 to promote revival of the Japanese aircraft industry. The government shouldered 50 percent of the equity and full subsidization of development expenses. The other cartel investors were simply the heavy industry corporations and instrument manufacturers that would be engaged in aircraft production. Cartels take several forms, and some, such as NAMC, take the form of individual corporations.[33]

Recent computer projects also illustrate how Japanese cartels work. In 1975, to step up lagging development under earlier arrangements, the Japanese government set up the Very Large Scale Integration Development Association (VLSI), to develop large-scale integrated circuit technology. Forty percent of funds came from government, 60 percent from industry. Funds and research tasks went to MITI's Electronics Research Institute and NTT's Central Telecommunications Laboratory. They also went to two groups of corporate laboratories, the first consisting of Fujitsu, Hitachi, and Mitsubishi and the second of NEC and Toshiba. Results from all these labs then went to MITI's Central Laboratory, and from there to all manufacturers. MITI, in creating a cartel, simply brings together all the resources it needs for the purpose at hand, rather like a commander forming a task force.[34]

The Japan Electronic Computer Company is another instructive case. It was set up by MITI in 1961 to counter IBM's preeminence in world computer markets. It was jointly owned by the six major computer producers, Fujitsu, Hitachi, NEC, Toshiba, Mitsubishi, and Oki. Marie Anchordoguy has called it "quasi-private": private in form but set up by public authorities to use public funds for a public purpose. JECC, according to Anchordoguy, "has no sales division, only a few hundred employees, and at best earns profits of $1 to $2 million a year."[35]

JECC is a typical passthrough company, controlling prices of a commodity by buying and selling it on paper. In this case it raises prices to makers and lowers prices to users simultaneously in order to induce rapid increases in production. The difference, namely the large subsidy to makers, was made up in the form of $2 billion of below-market-rate long-term loans from the Japan Development Bank and city banks.[36]

JECC is a price cartel and private in form as distinct from the VLSI Development Association, which is a research cartel, joint government and private in form. Like all cartel creations, however, JECC is oriented to a specific set of tasks and is precisely fashioned to serve those tasks.

Mediating Levels of Strategic Coordination

There are in the Japanese economic system two middle echelons of coordination. The higher is MITI's industrial bureaus, such as MIIB, and the equivalent bureaus in other ministries. The second mediating level is that of neo-zaibatsu, industrial associations, and cartels.

Conventional market economists as a rule do not have too much to say about such mediating levels of strategic coordination. This is not the case for modern analysts of Anglo-American strategic institutions, however. For the latter, all these seemingly esoteric matters may be instantly familiar, and about as mysterious as apple pie. Despite their seeming complexity, these methods are business as usual to Western students of force structure. Strategic military systems, broadly speaking, use two kinds of command chains at all times: operational commands, which are mixed, and service (or branch) commands, which are homogeneous. Military systems often create a third kind of command, task forces, which are tailored and temporary. Japan's strategic economic system also has evolved these three types of mediating coordination echelon: the neo-zaibatsu, the industrial association, and the cartel, respectively.

The Japanese system in its mediating levels uses noninterventionist methods of coordination. This is a kind of noncoercive command, which is more lenient than that found in military systems at analogous levels, since it largely relies, rather like defense-related research, on lucrative funding incentives and on discipline accomplished by an environment of competitive rivalry. These "soft" command methods are nonetheless sufficient to allow MITI to effectively determine the outcome.

Mediating levels practice only creative, or nonobstructive, rivalry. This, too, is a common attribute of modern military systems. Two Marine divisions fighting side by side are aggressive, competitive, and efficient. Yet they coordinate constantly and carefully such that they never intentionally fire upon each other, which is both a measure and a source of their efficiency. They compete at engaging the mission, not each other. The meticulous coordination that is universal among strategic corporations in Japan is conceptually analogous to that required in modern military systems.

Original Genius

The only part of the Japanese system that is fully original may be this application of the basic devices of mediating levels of strategic coordination to the world of industry in the form of neo-zaibatsu, industrial associations, and cartels. Government economic planning per se is not new. Nor are publicly owned corporations. Nor are middle levels of strategic coordination in the military. But the distinctive Japanese arrangements at middle levels between the government and *economic* corporations are new. The mediating institutions are fluid, are autonomous for most purposes, and function at several levels. They are ingenious. They exist to achieve the impossible task of harmonizing coordination at the top with spontaneity at the bottom, and they do. They make it possible, in effect, for Japan to enjoy the benefits of planned growth and of free markets simultaneously.

The Japanese system is characterized by multilevel staffs practicing "soft" methods of command. There is an urgent logic to this. There are many sectors in modern society in which the public may feel it is necessary or desirable to impose policy objectives: military, agriculture, industry, finance, religion, education, research, communications, and so on. Each sector has its own qualities and its own genius. Naturally the forms of policy imposition must vary from sector to sector for optimum results. More specificity of policy coordination is needed in military affairs, where large numbers of persons must cooperate on the same operation for good results. Less specificity of policy instruction, indeed only the loosest of general mandates, is needed in a public university system, where research succeeds best when practiced by undistracted individual scholars. Theoretically, the degree of specificity of policy advice needed for techno-industrial production would lie somewhere between these two cases. The Japanese genius is that Japan has actually developed practical structures for providing policy direction of this optimal sort for industry.

"Soft" command may be thought of as the quality of command that is appropriate for industrial affairs, as distinct from military affairs, educational affairs, or any other sector's affairs. Soft command superimposes the public's will on the techno-industrial system. It does this, however, without jeopardizing the suppleness or impairing the spontaneous inventiveness that is essential to that system's successful performance. Japan has devised an original system to articulate national policy goals to autonomous productive corporations with a minimum of coercive intervention. In sum Japan has developed workable middle levels of coordination for strategic industry, an extraordinary feat.

Notes

1. Joseph A. Schumpeter, *Capitalism, Socialism and Democracy* (New York: Harper and Row, 1975 [1942]), p. 175.

2. Alfred D. Chandler, *Strategy and Structure* (Cambridge, MA: MIT Press, 1962).

3. Charles J. McMillan, *The Japanese Industrial System* (Berlin: Walter de Gruyter, 1984), pp. 65, 82; James Abegglen, "The Economic Growth of Japan," *Scientific American* 222.3 (Mar 70): 31–37, p. 35, cited in Marie Anchordoguy, *Computers, Inc.: Japan's Challenge to IBM* (Cambridge, MA: Harvard Council on East Asian Studies, 1989), p. 11.

4. See also Organization for Economic Cooperation and Development, *The Industrial Policy of Japan* (Paris: OECD, 1972), p. 57, for objectives of reconstruction by MITI; and Ira C. Magaziner and Thomas M. Hout, *Japanese Industrial Policy* (Berkeley, CA: Institute of International Studies, 1980), p. 48.

5. Ezra F. Vogel, *Japan as Number One* (New York: Harper and Row, 1979), p. 72.

6. For examples of mergers, see Chalmers Johnson, *Japan's Public Policy Companies* (Washington, DC: American Enterprise Institute, 1978), p. 59. For reduction of Japanese electronic calculator makers from 23 firms to 9, 1970 to 1985, see James C. Abegglen and George Stalk, *Kaisha* (New York: Basic Books, 1985), p. 53.

7. Richard E. Caves and Masu Uekusa, "Industrial Organization," pp. 459–523 in Hugh Patrick and Henry Rosovsky eds., *Asia's New Giant* (Washington, DC: Brookings Institution, 1976), p. 488.

8. *Tsusho sangyo roppo* [*International Trade and Industry Laws*], Tsusho sangyo-sho ed. [MITI ed.] (Tokyo: Marui Kobunsha, 1988), pp. 249–50, 266–84. Most of the industrial structure laws appear to be under the Industrial Policy Bureau's jurisdiction. See *Tsusan handobukku* [*MITI Handbook*], Tsusan handobukku henshu iinkai ed. [MITI Handbook Editing Committee ed.] (Tokyo: Shokokaikan, 1989) [hereafter *MITI Handbook*], p. 527.

9. One such agency is the Current Force Design and Modernization Directorate, Combined Arms Combat Development Activity, Training and Doctrine Command, U.S. Army.

10. McMillan, p. 291; Michael Gerlach, "*Keiretsu* Organization in the Japanese Economy," pp. 141–74 in Chalmers Johnson, Laura D'Andrea Tyson, and John Zysman eds., *Politics and Productivity* (New York: Ballinger, 1989), pp. 153–54.

11. Several observers have noted that Japanese corporations cooperate at some things and compete at others. See, for example, John Zysman's description of "controlled competition" among Japanese corporations in his *Governments, Markets, and Growth* (Ithaca, NY: Cornell University Press, 1983), p. 237.

12. Eleanor M. Hadley, *Antitrust in Japan* (Princeton, NJ: Princeton University Press, 1970), p. 258.

13. Gerlach, "*Keiretsu* Organization," pp. 145, 146–49.

14. Ibid.; Alexander K. Young, *The Sogo Shosha: Japan's Multinational Trading Companies* (Boulder, CO: Westview Press, 1979), p. 38.

15. Gerlach, "*Keiretsu* Organization," pp. 146–49; Young, pp. 39–41.

16. Gerlach, "*Keiretsu* Organization," pp. 145–47.

17. Ibid., pp. 150–51; McMillan, p. 241.

18. Gerlach, "*Keiretsu* Organization," pp. 150, 152–65.

19. See ibid., pp. 152–56 for internal lending patterns.

20. Ibid., pp. 156–62. Gerlach notes that the newer bank group neo-zaibatsu, Daiichi and Sanwa, have lesser magnitudes of crossholding than the 60 percent that characterizes the older neo-zaibatsu, being in the range of 30 to 40 percent. It is perhaps safe to assume, however, that even these lesser magnitudes represent secure controlling interest and that these groups are managed insofar as possible on the same pattern as are the longer-established prewar groups. See in this connection especially ibid., p. 159.

21. Ibid., p. 160.

22. *MITI Handbook*, pp. 815–17.

23. For a list of the associations affiliated with each individual bureau, see ibid., pp. 762–963.

24. See Magaziner and Hout, p. 44; and Leonard Lynn and Timothy J. McKeown, *Organizing Business: Trade Associations in America and Japan* (Washington, DC: American Enterprise Institute, 1988), pp. 13, 15, 26.

25. See, for example, Magaziner and Hout, p. 59.

26. Ibid., p. 45.

27. Ibid., p. 44.

28. For joint purchase of raw materials by the Japan Iron and Steel Federation, for example, see Lynn and McKeown, p. 42.

29. See Lynn and McKeown, pp. 14, 39–40; Hadley, p. 373. For the beef import case of 1989, see "Japanese Beef Importers," *Wall Street Journal*, July 28, 1989, p. A3.

30. Hadley, pp. 367–68, 370, 373, 378–79.

31. Ibid., pp. 377, 380–81; Caves and Uekusa, p. 487.

32. Clyde V. Prestowitz, *Trading Places* (New York: Basic Books, 1988), p. 221.

33. Richard J. Samuels and Benjamin C. Whipple, "Defense Production and Industrial Development: The Case of Japanese Aircraft," pp. 275–318 in C. Johnson L. Tyson, and J. Zysman, *Politics and Productivity*, p. 277.

34. Magaziner and Hout, pp. 103–04.

35. Anchordoguy, pp. 59–63; Magaziner and Hout, p. 105.

36. Anchordoguy, p. 59; Magaziner and Hout, p. 105.

3
Banks and Policy Companies: Market Conformity

MITI HAS THREE major levers of implementation: strategic instruction, orchestration of the flow of major funds, and orchestration of the price and distribution of certain important materials. We have already examined the mediating institutions of strategic instruction, namely neo-zaibatsu, industrial associations, and cartels. Orchestration of the flows of funds and materials is also achieved through mediating levels of institutional organization. To regulate the flow and price of funds, MITI (and MOF) relies on the banking system, the Postal Savings System, the insurance system, the tax system, and prices of government-influenced quasi-public goods such as rail transportation and energy. Regulation of the price and distribution of important materials is achieved through public policy companies. The Japanese genius at the mediating levels of strategic instruction is that MITI informs neo-zaibatsu of the strategic policy, then gets out of their way so they can implement it. Efficiency is required by the discipline of structural competition. Enthusiasm is encouraged by lucrative funding incentives. The ends are determined above, but the means are determined by autonomous corporations below. Planning in this mode does not inhibit the pluralist spontaneity of the corporations below.

Mediating institutions that govern the flow of major funds and certain materials also have an original genius that is a key to their success. They use "market conforming methods."[1] They create market conditions that foster policy goals, but they do so by mimicking conventional market participants. They thus may intervene without disrupting the normal functioning of the market. This method is important because it preserves the dynamism and energy of persons or institutions seeking to enrich themselves in the market. Planners can pursue policy goals in this way without abridging the market or asking anyone to ignore the market. They have the benefit of planning but also of the full power and vitality of the market. In other words, they appear to have solved the perplexing riddle of how to achieve a degree of policy intervention without impairing the fragile medium of the market.

The market-conforming institutions involved in this process, namely banks and PPCs, have the purpose of moving funds and materials, that is, essential factors of production, to strategic corporations so that they can expand production rapidly. This factor abundance is a kind of surge of social energy that allows the corporations to move smoothly and swiftly to the desired goal. This abundance, however, also has a powerful motivational effect. It creates a climate of interest in the operating corporations for growth. This is one of the elements that makes strategic instruction, noninterventionist command, possible. Participating corporations automatically become rich. This being so, coercion of corporations by planners is hardly necessary. Mere instruction is enough, given, of course, that massive funding routinely follows. Planners quietly communicate what they want, and corporate managers go charging off to do it, their morale and spontaneous voluntarism fully intact.

Orchestration of the Flow of Funds: Strategic Investment

Besides supervising the economy by direct instructions to neo-zaibatsu or industrial associations, the government orchestrates the economy by effectively determining large-scale flows of capital. The Japanese financial system is like a giant civil-engineering project that gathers up surplus capital in the society and channels it into one powerful current to nourish industrial growth. Historically, at least during the years of rapid growth, 1952–1973, 20 percent or more of Japan's GDP flowed through this system each year, savings destined for industry.[2] Transfer of a cornucopia of wealth to strategic industry each year was achieved by interactive elements of the banking system, as we shall see, and also by pronounced differentials in the tax system and price system.

Japanese planners have managed, by orchestrating funds flows, to achieve a remarkably high investment rate of savings in the techno-industrial sectors. This is possible because strictly private investment in these sectors has been largely replaced by some 33 financial institutions, all government-owned or government-influenced.[3] These main 33 financial houses are, as we shall see, the Bank of Japan, the Industrial Bank of Japan, the Japan Development Bank, the 6 non-neo-zaibatsu city banks, the 6 neo-zaibatsu city banks, the 5 neo-zaibatsu trust banks, and the 13 neo-zaibatsu insurance companies.

Strategic Orchestration of Funds:
The Banking System

The strategic banking system functions like a great reservoir that catches the financial rainfall in the valley of Japan, then channels it to favored industrial fields downstream. This part of the Japanese banking system does not function only as a convenience to depositors or to local interests that want to borrow. Rather it functions also to channel a major proportion of GDP to priority industries. Let us follow this powerful flow from its headwaters to the rich fields it finally irrigates. Capital is generated at the headwaters by the patient toil of 120 million people, who produce more than they consume. Personal savings rates, including savings rates by proprietors of small businesses, are among the highest in the world, averaging 20 percent of disposable income in the 1970s.[4]

According to Yoshio Suzuki, research official of the BOJ, Japanese personal savings in the five years 1970 to 1974 were 16 percent of GDP. But in addition to this, savings by industry were 14 percent of GDP, and savings by government 7 percent of GDP, a total of 37 percent of GDP. Of this amount, 21 percent of GDP was invested in industry, 11 percent in personal assets, and 5 percent in government assets. Industries invested 7 percent of GDP more than they saved; persons and governments invested 5 and 2 percent less, respectively. This shows that savings rates by individuals, corporations, and governments were all high. It shows also that the banking and tax systems served to transfer funds to industry from individuals and government. Savings and investment rates were higher in the years of rapid growth, 1952–1973, and a bit lower post-1973. However, even the lower rates of the 1970s showed a magnitude of 20 percent of GDP of annual investment in industry.[5] The real investment rates, especially in the years 1952 to 1973, may have been higher even than this because of additional major wealth transfer in the form of preferential taxes and in the form of preferential prices for transportation and energy.

Let us consider why individual and government savings rates are so high, and how these savings are directed to favored industries. (Why corporate savings rates are high will be considered in Chapter 4.) There are a number of structural reasons for high rates among individuals. There is almost no consumer credit, so Japanese craving an auto or other appliance must save the whole amount before purchase. There is little social security support for the aged, so persons in their peak earning years are encouraged to save at very high rates for retirement. All institutional workers experience structured savings in the form of "bonuses." A third of employees' pay, on average, is withheld and paid in two lump sums during the year. This accustoms workers to living on two-thirds of their pay and banking the rest.[6] There are also positive incentives to save. In the Postal Savings System, and until recently in the general banking system as well, interest received on personal bank deposits has been tax free. Besides that, banks themselves operate energetic savings programs whereby depositors "contract" with them to deposit so much per month, in effect installment saving. Bank representatives visit depositors who are late with their savings payments. For all these reasons, savings by individuals and small businesses in Japan are extremely high.[7]

Japanese savings end up disproportionately in banks because real property is often exorbitantly expensive, because stock and bond markets are comparatively undeveloped, and because appliances are high-priced due to wholesaling mark-ups and national excise taxes; the interest on bank deposits, however, is untaxed. Note that there just happen to be structural factors at each step of the process that cause capital to flow one way.

Having explored incentives to save, let us examine the routes by which this accumulating treasure is moved to strategic corporations. Theoretically, the simplest way to generate the funds needed for rapid growth in a system like Japan's might be to provide compelling incentives to save (described earlier), to require all savings institutions to make reserve deposits in the central bank equal to what is needed for growth, then to have the central bank lend these funds to competent investment banks on the basis of their past lending performance. Such a procedurally uniform system would be relatively easy to establish and operate (see Figure 3.1). The Japanese system is not this simple, of course, but does, by several different routes, at least four main ones, do complexly what the just-described theoretical system would do simply: move funds equal to a major proportion of GDP from small savers to strategic industries. All four of Japan's main routes of capital mobilization can be assimilated to this single theoretical model, and the model helps illustrate the logic of each mobilization pattern. Some routes do omit the stage of the savings banks, or the stage of the central bank, or both. None omits the stage of the competent investment banks, since these are necessary to effect a prudent final distribution of the major funds involved.

We must consider here the role of the Ministry of Finance (MOF) and the Bank of Japan (BOJ). The MOF, largely through the BOJ, which is administratively subordinate to it, supervises the whole financial flood, with the partial exception of that which passes through the Postal Savings System. The BOJ has extensive formal regulatory powers over bank interest rates, bank reserve requirements, and apparently also bank licensing, which determines whether a bank can do business, as well as the number and location of a bank's branches. These powers, along with the informal powers they most likely generate, allow MOF and BOJ effectively to shape and regulate the banking system.

Under the BOJ's watchful eye, the regional banks lend funds to the 12 city banks. The 64 regional banks are headquartered in the less urban prefectures. Some of their funds are lent to local individuals and small firms, since they, too, have investment needs. Some of the rest of their funds, however, are routed to the city banks, where they are available for distribution to strategic industry. It would be in

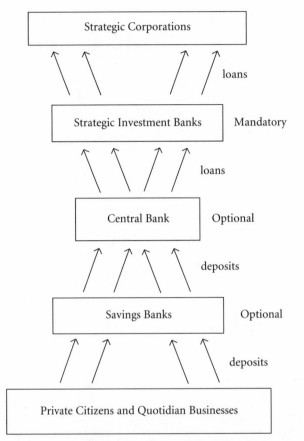

Figure 3.1 *A Simplified Theoretical Model for the Regulation of Funds Flows in Japan*

accord with the logic of this system if regional banks were required to keep reserve deposits with the BOJ, which could then be lent at the BOJ's preferred rates to the city banks, but it is not clear whether this actually happens (see Figure 3.2).[8]

Another route by which funds move from the citizenry to the strategic investment banks is through the BOJ itself (see Figure 3.2). The BOJ holds funds from a variety of sources, including revenues from taxes and fees, deposits from various government entities and public policy companies, and deposits from other banks. The BOJ itself lends funds to the 12 city banks. These funds are substantial, but their impact is more substantial still because they serve as an indicator of the government planners' desires. This is done through "window guidance," which means that when the borrower comes to the cashier's window, the cashier tells him what he must achieve with the funds. If the borrower fails to comply, the cashier may not have funds for him the next time. BOJ intends that the city banks

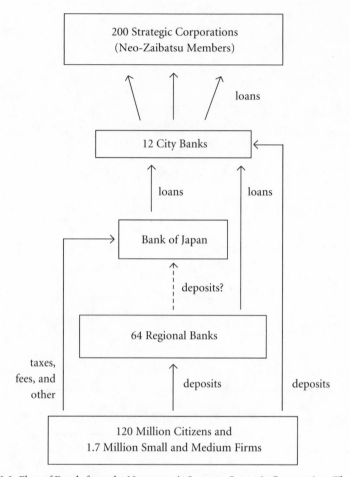

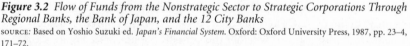

Figure 3.2 *Flow of Funds from the Nonstrategic Sector to Strategic Corporations Through Regional Banks, the Bank of Japan, and the 12 City Banks*
SOURCE: Based on Yoshio Suzuki ed. *Japan's Financial System.* Oxford: Oxford University Press, 1987, pp. 23–4, 171–72.

will add their own vast funds to priority projects identified through window guidance. The city banks are wise to do so because these are the projects that will be expedited in every way by government planners. Of course, bankers who ignore guidance also risk rousing the planners' ire in general, which in this system can have serious repercussions.[9]

The so-called city banks are Japan's 12 major strategic investment banks, the major financial engines of growth. They are Mitsubishi, Mitsui, Sumitomo, Fuji (Fuyo group, formerly Yasuda), Sanwa, and Daiichi, namely the six main banks closely associated with the neo-zaibatsu, and six others. It is only these banks, not the regional banks, that are franchised to operate branches in the financially flush urban areas. These 12 banks hold 60 percent of all Japan's bank deposits. They are themselves savings banks, with many branches to attract depositors, as well as investment banks. These banks move funds most directly of all from the quotidian economy to the strategic economy (see Figure 3.2). There are no intermediaries at all, though the BOJ monitors these funds' movements and still expects these movements to meet BOJ aspirations. More funds probably flow to the city banks by this route, direct deposit, than any other.

Because the city banks' purpose is to nourish growing industries, they are encouraged to lend out all the huge deposit assets they have, and then to lend out further the major funds they are continually borrowing from the BOJ, or the regional banks. They lend out all their own deposits, then borrow more from the BOJ and lend that. They lend more than they have got. Financial officials call this phenomenon "overloan." The 12 city banks' cash reserve position is actually negative at all times. The city banks are not conservative or reluctant to lend and are in fact very precariously leveraged by Western standards. They are the conduit by which the mighty rush of funds moves to strategic industries, not conservators.[10]

Despite the intrinsic boldness of their role, the 12 city banks have an important function as investment banks and are held responsible as investment banks. Within the policy parameters set by BOJ, they must pick winners and losers. They must judge which corporations can succeed at growth and so repay their loans from growth revenues. They rarely lend more than a few percent of their portfolios to any one firm, so as to spread their risk. This involves many and continuous fine judgements about the real capabilities of particular corporations. Making those judgements is a principle reason for the city banks' existence, and their hardest task. They compete with each other to do this, and with little margin for failure, since interest rates are kept artificially low. If they are not competitive in their decisionmaking, they can fail and go bankrupt, as the Sanwa Bank did in the late 1980s.

The city banks, like all institutions in the Japanese system, have destiny: the right to triumph and the right to fail, by their own deeds. The consequence for borrower corporations is that they must constantly impress scores of strategic lending institutions that they can succeed at growth. The 200 strategic corporations must compete among themselves to impress the investment banks. This imposes a rigorous performance discipline on them as well, but with no formal intervention as such from MOF or MITI. This is another case of Japanese reliance on what Johnson calls "market conforming methods." Discipline comes from competition in the market.

Just as city banks lend beyond their assets, so do the 200 strategic corporations borrow far beyond their collateral. Financial officials call this "overborrowing." Expanding corporations may borrow an amount equal to 30 percent or more of annual sales revenues, a percentage that would be considered imprudent in the West. Moreover, a disproportionate part of their externally obtained development capital comes from bank borrowing, over 90 percent in the high-growth years, according to Suzuki. One result is that 70 percent of the average Japanese corporation's capital is bank debt.[11]

The strategic corporations themselves are highly leveraged for the high purpose of rapid growth. They borrow far beyond their net revenues and repay with revenues from rapidly expanding capacity. Prestowitz cites the case of the Nippon Electric Company (NEC), which each year in the early 1980s invested an amount equal to 30 to 40 percent of its total semiconductor sales in new plant. In 1984 alone it increased production by 50 percent. This was possible because of heavy borrowing from city banks, and NEC was in fact leveraged at exactly the average rate for all Japanese corporations: 70 percent. Still, NEC could easily repay its huge debts because of the equally huge increases in production it was carrying out.[12] (The potential inflationary effect of no-reserve lending is evidently also overcome in this way: Bank credit increases the effective money supply, but expanded production provides more goods for this expanded money supply to chase.)

BOJ controls long-term interest rates and keeps them artificially low, that is, below the market rate, in order to accommodate long-term investment growth by the strategic corporations. This decreases their risk in borrowing and increases the proportion of wealth created over which the corporations can retain control. This means that capital is, however, rationed by BOJ and the city banks. It goes to the corporations that offer the best chance for strategic growth, not to the highest bidder. Of course, there is always more demand for funds at the artificially low rates than there are funds available. Tax exemption in some form is usually available for interest paid on growth capital, so that between the low rates and tax breaks, the real interest paid by strategic corporations on growth capital is extremely low. There is relatively little risk at such rates, and strategic corporations are in a constant clamor for this type of funds. Short-term funds, however, in amounts prescribed by BOJ regulations, are not controlled and move about the banking system freely at a much higher interest rate, whatever the market will bear.[13]

Funds that move from neo-zaibatsu city banks to strategic corporations are significantly augmented by funds that move to the strategic corporations through other neo-zaibatsu financial institutions (see Figure 3.3). Each neo-zaibatsu has a quartet of financial institutions to power growth: its main bank (which is one of the 12 city banks), a trust bank, a life insurance company, and a casualty insurance company. The main banks, trust banks, and life insurance companies lend funds to neo-zaibatsu member corporations, although it is not clear whether the casualty companies do. (Note also that Sanwa has no casualty company and that Daiichi has no trust bank but does have two casualty and two life insurance com-

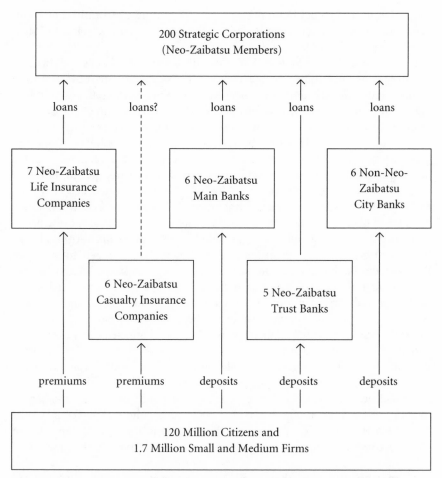

Figure 3.3 *Flow of Funds Through Neo-Zaibatsu Financial Institutions and City Banks*
SOURCE: Based on Michael Gerlach, "*Keiretsu* Organization in the Japanese Economy." Pp. 141–74 in Chalmers Johnson, Laura D'Andrea Tyson, and John Zysman, eds., *Politics and Productivity.* New York: Ballinger, 1989, pp. 145–47, 152–56.

panies. This means there are actually five neo-zaibatsu trust banks and seven life insurance companies, rather than six of each.)[14]

The neo-zaibatsu life insurance companies gather up capital the main banks might have missed. Like the city banks, the neo-zaibatsu insurance companies and trust banks receive funds directly as premiums or deposits from their own insurance clients or depositors, without BOJ or other intermediaries. As in the case of the city banks, these funds can then be channeled to the 200 strategic industrial corporations. The neo-zaibatsu financial institutions favor corporations in their own neo-zaibatsu group, but only marginally. All of these institutions make investment decisions independently and usually invest only a few percent of their funds in a given venture.[15]

Japan's Postal Savings System (PSS), like the neo-zaibatsu banks and financial institutions, is still another channel by which public savings are made to flow to strategic industries. The PSS is a remarkable phenomenon in itself. Post offices in Japan offer what is essentially a consumer banking service, with deposits, short-term lending, electronic funds transfers, long-term certificates of deposit, and other features. Twenty-three thousand neighborhood branches and tax-free interest on savings have brought into the PSS deposit assets three times larger than the largest city bank's. The system provides funds annually that are equal to about half of the Japanese national budget. Through MOF's Fiscal Investment and Loan Plan (FILP), these funds are allocated much as other government revenues are allocated.

Japanese planners tend to conceptualize bank deposits and taxes as being essentially the same thing: public savings that must be invested for the community's future well-being. PSS funds in the 1950s and 1960s flowed largely to the Japan Development Bank (JDB) for investment in priority industries. The Postal Savings System, through FILP, was thus in the 1950s and 1960s itself a financial engine of strategic industrial development, just as the BOJ, regional bank, and city bank systems were, and was operating parallel to them. The Postal Savings System collected billions of yen, as the other systems did, and channeled them to strategic corporations for development, albeit through the medium of MITI's JDB rather than through MOF's BOJ and the city banks (see Figure 3.4).[16] In the less frantically developmental 1980s, FILP expenditures from the PSS were shifted to housing, small business, environmental projects, and the like. Planners thus could spend more on these nondevelopmental things, but without losing control over how much was spent. Moreover, since this was the part of the banking system planners controlled most directly, they could easily shift funds back to the JDB if the need arose.[17]

There is financing available in Japan for nondevelopmental purposes in the quotidian consumer economy, through regional banks and other institutions, but this financing is provided only after developmental needs are met. The MOF and other ministries operate nearly a dozen financial corporations for small concerns: the Japan Housing Corporation; the Small Business Finance Corporation; the Agriculture, Forestry, and Fishery Finance Corporation; and the like. The government operates these agencies so that funds available to the everyday economy increase, but also, perhaps, to see to it that they do not increase too much.[18]

The object of the strategic banking system is to move vast funds, a major proportion of GDP, from the quotidian economy to the strategic economy. This movement depends in part on the financial altruism of depositors. Since the system cherishes market-conforming methods, however, this financial altruism of depositors is not forced and rather is induced with a small cash premium, namely the modest interest on their bank savings.

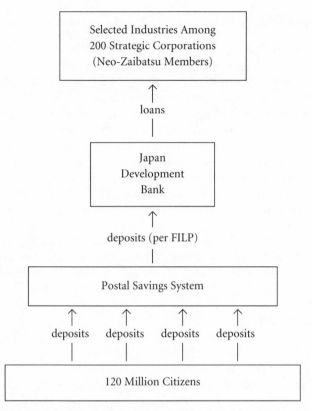

Figure 3.4 *Flow of Funds Through the Postal Savings System in the 1960s*
SOURCE: Developed from Kent E. Calder, "Linking Welfare and the Developmental State: Postal Savings in Japan." *Journal of Japanese Studies* 16.1 (Win 90): 31–59, p. 34.

There are four main routes by which funds move from the small everyday depositor to strategic investment banks, all four supervised by the MOF and the BOJ (the partial exception being the PSS, where other ministries participate). One route runs through the BOJ itself as loans to the 12 city banks. A second route runs through the 64 regional banks to the investment banks, either as loans or as deposits. A third route runs directly from the depositor to the city banks or other neo-zaibatsu financial institutions. A fourth route, not the least, runs through the PSS, FILP, and JDB. These routes, despite their apparent diversity, have largely the same purpose and effect.

The Japanese banking system may be thought of as a kind of mobilization system. It is fashioned so as to move liquidity in large and constant volume from 120 million savers to Mitsubishi Bank, and from there to Mitsubishi Heavy Industries. Moreover, since everything that is borrowed by corporations must be repaid to the city banks and to the BOJ, revenues from expanded plant return to the banks as a permanent, rapidly growing, ever-recycled investment fund.

Taxes and Prices

Wealth is gathered from all but lent mainly to favored corporations by the strategic banking system, as we have seen. The tax system and price system in Japan may also transfer wealth to these same favored corporations, however. Strategic industries, that is, industries given developmental priority by MITI, enjoy tax exemptions that may reduce their tax liability to near zero while they are engaged in rapid expansion. Like universities or churches in the United States, favored strategic industries enjoy major tax exemptions. Taxes in the aggregate amount to the price of government services in the aggregate. Since strategic industries are not paying this full price but are receiving the services, that means that the burden of paying for the government services these industries receive has been shifted to individual citizens and to nonstrategic small companies, a process similar in effect to a shift in funds.

Joseph Pechman describes the Japanese tax system as being active, meaning it is constantly adjusted to serve strategic purposes. Strategic taxes are all codified in the Special Tax Measures Law to distinguish them from the more mundane revenue-oriented tax provisions. There are over 50 "special" tax arrangements that are added to, deleted, or adjusted annually as development policy requires. Special taxes are arrived at by a three-way negotiation between MITI, MOF's Tax Bureau, and the Tax Advisory Commission, which is the Tax Bureau's advisory council. MITI planners determine which industries national policy interests require be helped, and with the Tax Bureau's concurrence, those industries obtain tax relief under the Special Tax Measures Law. The object of these exemptions is usually to promote rapid growth of production capacity but also to upgrade technology and increase export sales.[19]

Special tax measures characteristically include accelerated depreciation for important industrial equipment, additional initial depreciation for important industries, and deductions for income from export sales. In favored industries, depreciation schedules for new equipment are steep, often amounting to 50 percent or more of the equipment's value in the first year.[20] This means that half the cost of investment in plant can be exempted from the corporation's income taxes. Ryoshin Minami points out that for some industries, the government also pays the interest on capital borrowed for plant expansion, thereby providing the company with free capital.[21] There are, of course, many other tax methods besides the workhorse of special depreciation that allow MITI to move wealth to strategic industries: deduction of income from export sales, tax-free cash reserves for losses from export transactions, reduced taxes on stock dividends paid to strategic industries by companies they own, tax credits for increases in research and development outlays, and the like.[22]

This extraordinary tax largesse for expanding industries has not bankrupted the Japanese fisc, however. Far from it. Rapid industrial growth expanded the GDP, and thus also the tax base, by 10 percent per year in the years of rapid growth.

Therefore, tax yields from individual and corporate income taxes were growing 10 percent a year in real terms without any increase in the tax rates. Committed to lean government, the Tax Bureau reduced tax rates on both personal and corporate incomes almost every year between 1954 and 1974 yet still harvested large surpluses. Other categories of tax increased slightly from 1954 to 1974, however, keeping the whole tax burden nearly constant at just under 20 percent of GDP for the whole period, as compared with about 33 percent for the United States.[23] Growth since 1974 has been closer to 5 percent per year than 10, but even so, government expenditures on itself, as well as tax rates, have remained restrained.

The tax system, like the banking system, is so fashioned as to transfer wealth from the society at large to favored industries. Although there is less scholarly literature on this phenomenon in the West, certain basic prices regulated by the government also appear to mobilize wealth in a way similar to the tax system. Railroad transportation of heavy cargo is apparently available to strategic corporations at somewhat less than the real cost, the difference being born by other rail users, meaning mainly commuters and travelers. Electrical energy is apparently available to strategic industries at a much lower price than to household users. In other words, the population pays higher rates in order to provide energy and transportation at reduced rates to strategic corporations. Certain government-orchestrated price structures appear to channel wealth to favored strategic corporations as do the tax and banking structures explored earlier.

Orchestration of Materials Flow: Public Policy Companies

Besides strategic instruction and determination of major capital flows, MITI governs the strategic economy by regulating the flow of certain selected materials and products. It does this through a host of "public policy companies" (PPCs). Chalmers Johnson in his insightful study of these institutions describes and categorizes 112 major ones affiliated with the various ministries. The *MITI Handbook* lists some 1,100 PPCs and associations, major and minor, that are affiliated just with MITI. These structures are meant to serve all manner of purposes and are variously organized.[24]

A number of these PPCs are public monopolies. They are government-capitalized quasi-private corporations that buy all of a commodity that is produced and resell it. The entire commodity must pass through the PPC, albeit usually just on paper. These companies monopolize the movement of a particular material. The main purpose of most such companies is price regulation, to raise or lower a price if the market price may not achieve strategic goals. Public policy companies are independent of the market, yet they mimic the market to get the effects that they want.

PPCs: Developmental Prices

A special case of PPC is the developmental PPC, which raises prices to makers and lowers prices to users simultaneously. The best known case of this is probably the Japan Electronic Computer Company (JECC), but careful inquiry might disclose a number of others in the postwar period. The developmental PPC of the JECC type is sufficiently ingenious that it is worthy of closer scrutiny.

According to the law of supply and demand, the natural, equilibrium price is that where the typical supply and demand curves intersect, point x_0, y_0 (see Figure 3.5). This single point governs much: It determines how much of a commodity is produced, how much is consumed, how much is paid, and how much is received.

The purpose of a developmental PPC, however, is to increase production, that is, the number of items produced, to x_1, and incidental to this, to increase the number of items consumed to this same x_1 level (see Figure 3.6). The only way to achieve this without diluting market incentives is to pay the supplier more for x_1

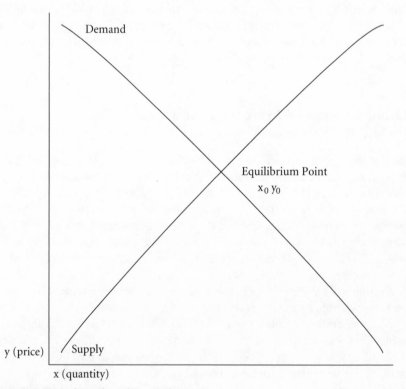

Figure 3.5 *Typical Supply and Demand Curve*
NOTE: Economists often call x_0, y_0 the equilibrium point.

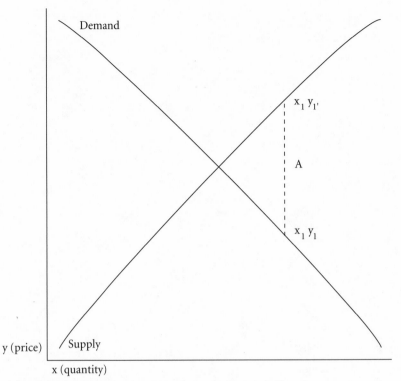

Demand

$x_1 y_{1'}$

A

$x_1 y_1$

y (price) Supply

x (quantity)

Figure 3.6 *Supply and Demand Curve with Development Subsidy*
NOTE: A equals the subsidy per item.

items than the demander is willing to pay (y_1') and at the same time to give the x_1 items to the demander for less than the supplier is willing to accept (y_1). This means the PPC is paying a subsidy (A) on each of the x_1 items.

The result is an uncoerced increase in production. Changing the prices in itself induces brisk compliance with MITI's plans. No other intervention is necessary. The PPC meanwhile operates at a loss, covered by funds from the JDB or some other MITI-controlled source. The subsidies are required only for a limited period because the producer, due to his having more funds to invest in production assets and due to economies of scale and his learning curve, is eventually able to reduce his prices to what the user will pay. That is, the marginal cost of production falls. The user meanwhile has become accustomed to mass consumption of the product. MITI can then shift its developmental funds to some other project. This is another case where MITI resourcefully relies on market methods to achieve strategic goals.

Where do these developmental PPCs' funds come from, however? They are not necessarily paid back, unlike funds received as loans from banks. The answer is

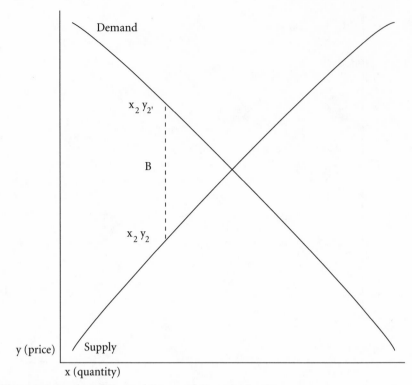

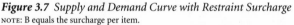

Figure 3.7 *Supply and Demand Curve with Restraint Surcharge*
NOTE: B equals the surcharge per item.

that the development-subsidy PPCs are matched by restraint PPCs that generate revenue, which is then available for development (see Figure 3.7). The restraint PPC, as a legal monopoly, buys all of the item produced at lower than the natural market price (y_2). This reduces the amount produced from x_0 items to x_2 items. It then sells x_2 items to demanders at more than the natural price (y_2'). This yields ongoing revenue of B for each item, which funds can then be used to offset the ongoing losses of the A subsidies.

This balance allows the PPC system as a whole to be revenue neutral and not to draw on bank funds or tax funds. Development PPCs withdraw funds from the JDB, but meanwhile restraint PPCs have put funds in. Another way to think of this is that the revenues generated by the restraint PPCs amount to an excise tax—collected by them, not by the MOF—whose proceeds are devoted to industrial development via the JDB. As long as all subsidies (A) are less than or equal to all surcharges (B), the planners can do all the subsidizing they want with no loss of funds. For certain products, market prices seem to have given way to developmental prices.

Development PPCs:
The Japan Electronic Computer Company

The most celebrated example of a development PPC in the Western literature in recent years is probably the Japan Electronic Computer Company (JECC). The JECC was created in 1961 under MITI auspices. It is a joint venture consisting of six computer producers: Fujitsu, Hitachi, NEC, Toshiba, Mitsubishi, and Oki. It has no sales division, has only a few hundred employees, and shows a profit of less than $2 million a year. Even so, it is a key to Japanese industrial dynamism in the 1990s.

Between 1961 and 1981, the Japanese government infused $2 billion into JECC in the form of low-interest loans funneled mainly through the JDB. These funds were used to purchase computers from the fledgling Japanese computer industry at a time when both production and consumption were at a low level and when high start-up costs made Japanese computers uncompetitive with their IBM counterparts. JECC purchased the computers at full price, cost plus profit, then rented the computers at rates lower than IBM's to Japanese corporate users. JECC paid more than the market price to producers and required less than the market price from users. This increased domestic production and consumption simultaneously but also made necessary the constant infusion of subsidized loans. In other words, the JECC was a quintessential development PPC.[25]

Restraint PPCs:
Gambling, Sugar, Tobacco

Restraint PPCs' main purpose seems to be to raise revenue for strategic development. They levy surcharges, however, only on activities or products where the government and public believe it is in the public's interest for the activity to flourish at a somewhat lesser level than the market left to itself would allow. These activities and products tend to be those for which user interest greatly outstrips production costs: gambling, sugar, tobacco, salt, alcohol. These are widely enjoyed, and high markups on them yield major revenues. In some cases, these revenues are assigned directly to the higher purpose of industrial development.

The Japanese public enjoys bicycle racing, motorcycle racing, boat racing, and horse racing. These racing activities are operated by local government authorities or their designated agents. Part of the proceeds are retained by local governments, and part are forwarded to the appropriate national supervisory organization. MITI supervises bicycle and motorcycle racing, the Ministry of Transportation looks after boats, and the Ministry of Agriculture and Forestry oversees the horses.

Bicycle racing is a lucrative pet preserve of MITI's elite Machine and Information Industries Bureau (MIIB). There are numerous PPCs in this MITI bureau associated with bicycles or bicycle racing.[26] Why should the cutting-edge development bureau have an interest in bicycle racing? In fact, these PPCs are restraint PPCs that generate off-line revenues that the MIIB can use for developmental projects. These funds are, of course, less scrutinized by the public than those that pass through the tax system or banks. The MIIB supervisory organization is the Japan Bicycle Promotion Association. Its purpose is "the promotion of industries related to machines." A similar system exists for motorcycle racing under MIIB's Japan Motorcycle Promotion Association.[27]

Over the past 30 years, the bicycle-racing system has generated $2 billion of revenue for MIIB, some of it handed over directly to the machine tool producers' associations, which are also in MIIB's stable of auxiliary institutions.[28] The racing corporations amount to a kind of excise tax system whose revenues flow, like those of banks and other taxes, to industrial development. They represent one way of offsetting the losses of development PPCs.

Besides gambling, another form of restraint PPC that generates revenue is the traditional monopoly. Sugar, tobacco, salt, and liquor monopolies generated a large proportion of the government's revenue before the war, and they still are major income sources. Especially noteworthy among these is the sugar monopoly, which in the period of rapid growth in the shipbuilding industry, the 1950s and 1960s, was assigned directly to the shipbuilders' manufacturing association. The sugar licenses produced major capital subsidies to shipbuilders much as bicycle racing did for machine tools in the 1980s.[29]

*   *   *

The orchestration of certain goods flows, like the orchestration of major funds flows, invigorates strategic industries while it restrains nonstrategic economic activity. The Japanese economic system is a blend of public and free-market elements so smooth that it outperforms most other systems. In the area of industrial investment, this blend entails leaving investment activity in the hands of expert investment bankers. The funds themselves, however, come mainly from publicly controlled bank deposits, not from private individual investors or portfolio-oriented institutions. The basic policies that guide these expert bankers come from the MITI and MOF officials who orchestrate the flow of funds received by the investment banks. Bankers are held responsible for their decisions and must seek to invest in firms that can and will repay the funds. Still, they must also invest compatibly with the nation's overall strategy for growth.

No modern public will tolerate public funds being used on a large scale for a private purpose. By determining the flow of bank funds, however, MITI and MOF officials see to it that industrial investment conforms to the public purpose. This feature of the system seems to have made it possible to mobilize public funds in substantial amounts for industrial investment. These funds in turn allow for industrial investment and growth on an unprecedented scale. Investment appears to actually be at a rate equal to about 20 percent of the nation's total annual GDP in ordinary years, and the rate was probably more in the rapid-growth 1960s.

Having all major capital funds professionally invested through the banking system but in accord with publicly established developmental priorities is another one of postwar Japan's resourceful blends of planning and implementational freedom. It allows the Japanese to overcome the puzzle of how to invest public funds in particular industrial corporations. In other words, since certain corporations have been drawn into a pattern of public responsibility whereby the public can be reasonably assured it will get value for its contribution, the public can accept the channeling of publicly controlled funds to these institutions in substantial amounts.

Japanese planners have also learned to efficiently influence prices. Through the instrument of quasi-private corporations with a legal monopoly on a given product, planners are able to offer different prices to producers and users, thereby artificially stimulating, or restraining, both production and consumption. They do not seek to alter prices by hopefully petitioning the millions of market participants to act against their interests or by rigidly coercing them either. Planners simply establish a legal monopoly corporation that, like any monopoly, can shape the price and distribution of the commodity. No one in the market is expected to make a decision contrary to his market interest. This sophisticated approach appears to make possible major intervention in the prices of certain goods without suspending or significantly disrupting markets. In fact, these methods depend on the market's vigor and power to generate their intended consequences.

Japanese planners use mediating institutions to intervene in markets, to exercise decisive influence over major movements of funds and of certain materials, and to govern prices of certain goods separately for producers and users, thereby also governing production rates. These ongoing interventions are, however, sophisticated rather than draconian. They are carefully blended into the normal functioning of the markets. Market dynamics are respected and needed by planners. They therefore intervene in certain markets, but by means of sophisticated instruments that apparently allow them to do so without significantly abridging or impairing the markets' functioning.

Notes

1. Chalmers Johnson uses this term. See his *MITI and the Japanese Miracle* (Stanford, CA: Stanford University Press, 1982), pp. 315, 317, 318.

2. Organization for Economic Cooperation and Development, *The Industrial Policy of Japan* (Paris: OECD, 1972), pp. 163, 165.

3. For a useful overview of the Japanese banking environment cf. Yoshio Suzuki ed., *Japan's Financial System* (Oxford: Oxford University Press, 1987), pp. 163–170.

4. Ibid., p. 12; Clyde V. Prestowitz, *Trading Places* (New York: Basic Books, 1988), p. 126.

5. Suzuki, pp. 12–13. Percentages of GDP in this paragraph are arrived at by using the percentages of each sector's investment (given by Suzuki on p. 13) and multiplying these by 16.5 over 44, that is, by .375. This procedure relies upon Suzuki's indication (p. 12) that the 44 percent of total investment achieved by the personal sector is equal to 16.5 percent of GDP.

6. Miyohei Shinohara, *Industrial Growth, Trade, and Dynamic Patterns in the Japanese Economy* (Tokyo: University of Tokyo Press, 1982), pp. 157–61.

7. Suzuki, pp. 77–80; Kent E. Calder, "Linking Welfare and the Developmental State: Postal Savings in Japan," *Journal of Japanese Studies* 16.1 (Win 90): 31–59, p. 44; Stephen J. Anderson, "The Political Economy of Japanese Saving," *Journal of Japanese Studies* 16.1 (Win 90): 61–92, pp. 64, 67.

8. Suzuki, pp. 24, 172.

9. Ibid., pp. 23–24, 171–72; Charles J. McMillan, *The Japanese Industrial System* (Berlin: Walter de Gruyter, 1984), p. 291.

10. Suzuki, pp. 23–24, 171–72; McMillan, pp. 290–91.

11. Prestowitz, pp. 167–68; Suzuki, *Financial System*, pp. 23–24.

12. Prestowitz, pp. 167–68.

13. Suzuki, p. 24.

14. Michael Gerlach, "*Keiretsu* Organization in the Japanese Economy," pp. 141–74 in Chalmers Johnson, Laura D'Andrea Tyson, and John Zysman eds., *Politics and Productivity* (New York: Ballinger, 1989), pp. 145–47, 152–56.

15. Ibid.

16. Calder, p. 34.

17. Chalmers Johnson, *Japan's Public Policy Companies* (Washington, DC: American Enterprise Institute, 1978), pp. 81–87; Calder, pp. 31–34; Anderson, pp. 66–67.

18. For the full array of the Japanese banking system, see Suzuki, pp. 163–70, 170ff.; and McMillan, pp. 286–87.

19. Joseph A. Pechman, "Taxation," pp. 317–82 in Hugh Patrick and Henry Rosovsky eds., *Asia's New Giant* (Washington, DC: Brookings Institution, 1976), pp. 328, 329, 352–53.

20. Pechman, pp. 352–54; John Zysman, *Governments, Markets, and Growth* (Ithaca, NY: Cornell University Press, 1983), p. 242; Ira C. Magaziner and Thomas M. Hout, *Japanese Industrial Policy* (Berkeley, CA: Institute of International Studies, 1980), p. 70.

21. Ryoshin Minami, *The Economic Development of Japan* (London: Macmillan Press, 1986), p. 354.

22. Pechman, pp. 352–57.

23. Ibid., pp. 323–24. For the U.S. figure, see for example pp. 3–5 of "USA Statistics in Brief 1986," supplement to *Statistical Abstract of the United States 1986*, U.S. Dept. of Commerce ed. (Washington, DC: USGPO, 1985).

24. See C. Johnson, *Policy Companies*; and *Tsusan handobukku* [*MITI Handbook*], Tsusan handobukku henshu iinkai ed. [MITI Handbook Editing Committee ed.] (Tokyo: Shokokaikan, 1989) [hereafter *MITI Handbook*,], pp. 582–1077.

25. Marie Anchordoguy, *Computers, Inc.: Japan's Challenge to IBM* (Cambridge, MA: Harvard Council on East Asian Studies, 1989), pp. 59–60. For comprehensive treatment of the JECC, see ibid., pp. 59–91.

26. *MITI Handbook*, pp. 574, 896–904.

27. Cf. ibid., pp. 896–904, 854–56; Prestowitz, p. 221.

28. Machine tool PPCs under MIIB include the Japan Machine Tool Builders Association and the Machine Tool Engineering Foundation. See *MITI Handbook*, p. 803; Prestowitz, pp. 221–22.

29. On sugar imports being assigned to the shipbuilding industry, see Tuvia Blumenthal, "The Japanese Shipbuilding Industry," pp. 129–60 in Hugh Patrick ed., *Japanese Industrialization and Its Social Consequences* (Berkeley: University of California Press, 1976), p. 144.

4
Strategic Corporations: Public Production

$\mathbf{T}$O IMPLEMENT strategic production objectives, the Japanese system relies on an institution that to many Anglo-Americans may seem unique: the strategic corporation. There are about 200 of these, the 187 neo-zaibatsu members and some dozen other corporations such as Toyota and Toshiba that have sufficient revenues from export sales that they are less dependent for funds on the neo-zaibatsu banking groups. This export-manufacture type of firm produces a narrow range of consumer goods, not producers' goods, which also reduces its need to interact with neo-zaibatsu partners. These 200 strategic corporations, mostly neo-zaibatsu members, lie just below the neo-zaibatsu banks and presidents' clubs, industrial associations, and cartels in the system of strategic coordination.

The purpose of the strategic corporations is operational; that is, they are supposed to actually implement production policy. The echelons above, MITI and the industrial associations, are planning echelons. They develop plans and communicate them to the corporations. It is the strategic corporations, though, that must finally step through the looking glass and turn these hopeful plans into reality.

In order to orchestrate rapid capacity growth and other policy goals, economic planners require several qualities in the implementing institutions. They must be willing to accept the policy guidance from above and not be distracted. They must be ambitious and flexible in order to respond to the bonanza of opportunity the government opens to them. That is, they must be collectively energetic and resourceful. Planners need to be confident when they channel public capital into a company for the purpose of rapidly doubling its production that the production will in fact be doubled and that the precious funds under their stewardship will not instead flow ineffectually into the hands of external materials dealers, suppliers, wholesalers, or anyone else.

These companies, to be worthy of receiving the sacred elixir of public capital, must have no external leaks. Moreover, the companies must have no internal leaks. They must be lean such that public funds are all converted into new plant and technology, not merely distributed among company employees. Without implementing institutions that are lean and responsive, all MITI's grand plans would remain a dead letter. What, then, are these implementing corporations like?

The Strategic Corporation as Production Agency

Anglo-American observers tend to think of Japanese corporations as being essentially like manufacturing corporations in the United States or England. Japan's strategic corporations differ in some important respects from their Anglo-American counterparts, however. One way of approaching these differences is by thinking of these corporations as being a kind of public institution. Thus viewed, their marvels become somewhat more comprehensible. In many details of policy, governance, structure, financing, personnel, and the like, these corporations seem to more nearly resemble some elite public institutions in the West, such as those for education and research, or for defense.[1]

Is the strategic corporation public or private? The answer to this query is a bit elusive. The typical strategic corporation issues stock but is not controlled by stockholders. It seems to serve the national purpose but is not nationalized. A growing number of Western observers have come to believe that in the great Japanese corporations, the body of employees as a whole, but especially the upper levels of employees, actually conduct the affairs of these companies, with reference mainly to the interests of the institution but also to public policy directives from above.[2]

This pattern of elite self-governance in the public purpose might seem unusual were it not for the apparent fact that many institutional activities in the West defined as in the public purpose rely on some variant of this same system. Many demanding public activities in the West are entrusted to self-governing corps of vocationalized professionals. The only thing that differs in the Japanese case is that the Japanese have apparently decided that certain categories of industrial production fall within the public purpose. They therefore seem to have imposed on production some of the same standards of responsibility, meaning both autonomy and accountability, that are sometimes found in the context of other public activities. Given this proviso, the Japanese methods may not be as exceptional as they at first look.

Japan's strategic corporations are not public in the sense of being nationalized. They are, however, expected to be responsive to policy needs and to receive publicly controlled bank funds and major public subsidies. They observe extensive financial disclosure laws, a fairly common practice in Japan and elsewhere for institutions receiving public funds.[3]

Interownership and Managerial Autonomy

We have seen that a controlling proportion of each neo-zaibatsu member corporation's stock is cross-held by its fellow member corporations, in a magnitude of about 60 percent of stock outstanding for the older neo-zaibatsu. Even much of the fraction of stock that is not cross-held by members of the same neo-zaibatsu is stably held by members of other neo-zaibatsu or held by other large corporations and not traded. Eighty percent of Japan's largest companies' stocks are stably held.[4] Dividends are virtually guaranteed but are modest in amount. In practice only miniscule amounts of dividends are paid to stockholders who are not themselves other strategic corporations. Dividends mean only that several times a year these companies exchange modest checks of like amount. Relatively little wealth is lost to the system. It might be viewed as being more of a ritual gift exchange defining a relationship than a wealth transfer.

It is nearly impossible under prevailing conditions for stockholders outside the orbit of the neo-zaibatsu to acquire controlling interest in a strategic corporation by buying traded stock. In the rare cases where this has happened, as in the Asahi Breweries case or the Minebea case, the group bank or parent company has firmly intervened to rescind external acquisition. Collective self-ownership among neo-zaibatsu corporations may not be an accident of the market. It is apparently an institutional norm, maintained as a matter of policy.[5]

Individuals who hold strategic corporations' stock are customarily not very assertive. Stockholders' meetings are generally perfunctory. Even institutional holders of strategic corporations' stock differ fundamentally from the institutional holders of United States corporations' stock in that in the United States, two-thirds of institutional holders are pension funds or trust funds whose object, like that of individual investors, is portfolio returns. Their main object is often to transfer revenues from the held company to themselves. Almost all institutional holders in Japan, however, are other strategic corporations whose main interest is merely in the held company's prospering.[6]

Crossholding of stocks by strategic corporations means in practice that management is nearly autonomous.[7] There is apparently no major functioning ownership interest separate from management. Young traces this to the "management revolution" of 1946, when U.S. occupation officials ordered zaibatsu families to sell all their controlling shares in zaibatsu firms, which were then purchased by those very firms. Corporate stocks became interowned by groups of managers. Soon afterward, in 1950, a change in the commercial code formalized the tendency toward manager autonomy by reducing the power of individual stockholders vis-à-vis professional managers. This suggests that managerial autonomy in favored corporations may be a matter of law as well as custom.[8]

The Purposes of Stock Crossholding

Strategic corporations may be thought of as "quasi-private." They maintain some of the forms of privateness, though in organization and function they are in important respects public. So why do Japanese leaders not end this elaborate exhibition of private stockholding, or at least simplify the complex interholding pattern? It is perhaps paradoxical, but the forms of private stockholding efficiently serve several purposes that are essential to a responsive strategic system. One vital purpose of the stock is to define the mutually supportive relationships that exist among firms. It is crucial for defining neo-zaibatsu membership. Several U.S. observers use the term "symbolic" to describe this function. The stock symbolizes the relationship, rather than being held for capital gains per se. "Shareholding is the mere expression of their relationship, not the relationship itself," as one observer put it. In other words, the stock is held to give mutual testimony to the relationship, not for capital gains.[9]

A second purpose of private stockholding is to affirm the autonomy of the strategic corporations vis-à-vis the government and so thwart the government's tendency to micromanage. Flexibility and spontaneity below, pluralism in the public purpose, is the sine qua non for strategic industries' success. Without this, the system might become a dead monolith and fail, like the old Soviet Russian system. The existence of the stock provides a legal and formal basis for the companies' resisting government intervention in their internal operations.

At the same time, the strategic industries have what, in a sense, is the opposite problem. A group of people forming an agency will rarely function well unless they are in an environment of accountability. Even the most dedicated managers will perform infinitely better if they believe they will enjoy tangible and intangible rewards if they succeed, but forfeit such rewards if they do not. In sum, they have to be and feel accountable if the system is to be dynamic. Yet how can they be held accountable without disturbing their autonomy and spontaneity?

The solution to this conundrum is analogous to academia's solution: peer review. Each corporation's corps of managers is judged by the corps of managers of other corporations in the same neo-zaibatsu group. These bands of managers judge each other. Overseeing all this is the management group of the neo-zaibatsu bank. A corporation's management is accountable to other corporations in its group, the whole group then being supervised by the group bank.

Mutual stockholding formalizes this solution of peer review. Each corporation's management is in a formal sense accountable to stockholders, but the stockholders are in fact none other than peer corporations' managements. The practical effects of this can be seen in the flow of funds. If a neo-zaibatsu group is healthy, the BOJ will provide its bank with funds, and if a neo-zaibatsu member corporation is healthy, the neo-zaibatsu bank will provide it with funds. If a member corporation clearly fails, however, the group bank will stop providing funds and in fact intervene, take it over.[10]

Crossholding of stocks, as opposed to outright corporate self-ownership, is extremely useful for inculcating in managers this awareness that although autonomous in running their businesses, they are still responsible for good results and will lose their funds and freedom if they fail. Crossholding thwarts government meddling. Having freed managers from control by government, however, crossholding re-imposes on them a rigorous accountability to each other. The seeming needlessly elaborate crossholding does much to solve this riddle of how to set managers free yet still hold them accountable.

The forms of private stockholding are thus retained for strategic corporations because they help define relationships among neo-zaibatsu members and because they allow managers to be free of government meddling yet still be held accountable. The precise arabesque of interfirm stockholding is extremely useful for meeting some of the competing demands implicit in a strategic economic system, which by its nature requires coordination above and spontaneity below.

The Board of Directors

The strategic corporation's highest policy decisions are made by a committee consisting of its president, division heads, and other senior managers. These are the organization's senior statesmen. When convened as the policymaking committee, these senior employees are referred to as being the firm's "board of directors." Japan's strategic corporations do not have any board of directors in the Western sense of persons elected by external stockholder interests to supervise top management. Instead, the strategic corporation's board merely is its top management. This is more what one might expect of an elite self-governing corps of operatives running a public instruction. The corporation is run by its own senior statesmen, its own deans and presbyters.

Almost all "directors" are internal directors, that is, senior employees of the corporation. They are not chosen by stockholders and need not own any stock. The exception is that many neo-zaibatsu corporations have one or two directors, not more, who are senior officials or emeritus officials of another corporation in their group, of a senior financial institution, or of some corporation they work closely with; for example, heavy industries may trade directors with steel. The single external director obviously cannot do much specific supervising. His job is to communicate the senior corporation's expectations to the member corporation's board. The external director represents the accountability factor in intra-neo-zaibatsu relations.

Top management does not have to serve under a board of directors. Top management is the board. This enlivens morale throughout the company. Every new professional employee knows that he may end his career as a prestigious director of his own company. Every new employee carries a director's top hat in his briefcase.[11]

The Company President

The president of a strategic corporation is normally recruited from among the senior professional employees after a lifetime of service to the institution. The position of president tends to be ceremonial, however, not one of operational control. He represents the corporation in ceremonial activities and in contacts with other corporations and the public. If the corporation suffers a serious financial loss or commits some other faux pas, he will publicly assume responsibility and step down as a gesture of apology on behalf of the company. Real operational control, however, lies in the circle of top managers near him, vice presidents and department heads. Some decisions are made by consensus in lower echelons still.[12]

Presidents' pay is comparatively modest. According to Abegglen, after-tax compensation of chief executives in 1980 was 7.5 times that of new employees. This modest ratio is not too different from the salary ratio one finds in a U.S. university between a university president and a new assistant professor or in a military division between a major general and a new second lieutenant. These similarly modest ratios are, of course, very different from those of U.S. private corporations, where chief executives' pay ratios to new employees, are much higher.[13] The Japanese president does get a bonus, but it is identical as a proportion of salary to what every other employee gets. He is not paid in stocks and options. That is, he is not given personal property in the company.

The Japanese president of a strategic corporation appears to be regarded as a public servant, like a chancellor or an admiral. For a vocationalized professional person at the height of his career, successful in the public purpose, a large wealth transfer from his institution would be unnecessary, and, of course, might diminish the admiration he enjoyed among his colleagues and the public.

Professional Employees

Professional employees of strategic corporations, like much else in strategic corporations, differ greatly from their Anglo-American counterparts. They are hired only after careful scrutiny on a basis of character and overall intelligence, not on a basis of particular skills. The most prestigious strategic corporations hire from the same national universities drawn upon by the elite government bureaucracy, producing "university cliques" (*gakubatsu*). They hire at entry level only, like the military. They almost never hire at mid-career.[14]

Once hired, the corporation professional enjoys extraordinary advantages. He is given a near absolute guarantee of career security for life, and more. Because promotion in rank and pay is nearly automatic on a basis of seniority, he is guaranteed to rise continuously in the company. From the first day, the new employee is practically guaranteed professional success, a lifetime of recognition and fulfilled career hopes.[15]

The employee enjoys a cornucopia of other advantages: company housing, vacation facilities on mountain or shore, commuting subsidies, health insurance, family allowances, free classes in foreign languages or flower arranging, and organized sports activities, to name some. Rodney Clark maintains that company housing expresses "the solicitous attitude ... a successful firm should adopt toward its employees" and that it contributes to the sense of community in the company. Prestowitz notes in this vein that the Japanese company "is run to give purpose to the lives of those whom it employs."[16]

It is probably safe to assume that the object of providing career security, automatic promotion, and numerous other benefits is to foster several advantageous effects. Such benefits free the professional from many private worries so he can focus on his vocation. They provide a sense of gratitude in quid pro quo terms. They create a sense of collective pride among those receiving these benefits, which both defines the corporate community and raises collective morale. Moreover, these arrangements convey the message that the company cares, which perhaps makes the individual's burden of service seem lighter. His sacrifices on the company's behalf are self-affirming, not self-diminishing. The benefits allow the professional to justify investing more of himself.

Professional Self-Governance

Professional operatives of Japanese strategic corporations have another advantage their Anglo-American counterparts do not. They are collectively self-governing. They are fully franchised institutional citizens. They can savor a degree of what can fairly be called institutional democracy. They, in their collective capacity as the company, are free from direct interference from the outside (unless they fail); and in their capacity as individual professionals they have more voice and influence in their company's affairs than most Western employees do. Observers of this phenomenon declare that the Japanese corporation is run by "communal control from within companies" or that "big businesses in Japan today are almost completely under control by managers."[17] What all this amounts to is that professionals serving in strategic corporations are not exactly employees in the Western sense but rather are an elite self-governing corps of vocationalized operatives. They are more like professors or Marines.

Direct democracy might be ungainly in a large institutional setting. Pure authoritarianism might lead to a counterproductive rigidity. Virtually all modern institutions that work ingeniously intermix these two principles of governance. Formally, that is, by corporate regulation, Japanese corporations are governed hierarchically by the company president and his subordinates. Informally, and as a practical matter, many decisions are made collectively and at lower levels. In general, participants in a given decision are those who are informed about it and have a legitimate interest in it. Not all persons participate in all decisions. Employees at different levels participate in different levels of decision. Managerial employees only begin to take part in policy decisions after 10 to 15 years of service.

There are several processes by which collective wishes at a lower level become adopted as policy at a higher. The most formal and most famous of these is the *ringi* system. A *ringi* is a proposal generated by a manager or department and circulates among collateral departments and then among the company's senior managers, directors, and the president. Those who read the proposal comment on an attached form. When it reaches the president, he decides to implement the proposal or reject it. In practice, if the proposal enjoys widespread support, the president often will enact it. The *ringi* system is viewed by many as meaning that important decisions in the company are being made collectively by professional employees in lower echelons.[18]

There are other major indicators of democratic dynamics in Japanese corporate governance. In a typical company, there is a generous information flow in the form of *ringi*, daily pep talks, meetings, directives from the board, and the like. Great attention is paid to official instructions, regulations from the president, directives from the board, departmental instructions, factory regulations, and factory instructions issued at different levels and with different degrees of authority. The effect of all this information flow is not only that staff members are better-informed of their institution's affairs. It is also that each professional worker knows he is worth informing, which improves morale.[19]

Even when decisions originate at upper levels, they are floated at meetings, and efforts are made to get comments and approval at all levels of management. If a decision meets with derision or if it is obvious it would not be well-received, upper management often abandons or modifies it.[20] This pattern suggests that power is shared between higher officials lifted from the ranks because of superior capabilities and the whole institutional public, namely all professional employees of the company. In any case, placing final responsibility in the hands of relatively few higher officials gives this system policy coherence and requires that someone finally blend the many competing voices of the corporate democracy into one.

The strategic corporation seems to have some of the elements of an in-house democracy that an elected legislature or a university faculty normally has. One category of activity exempted from democratic processes, however, is personnel decisions. These are made in a briskly bureaucratic way with no group participation.[21]

Limits of Professional Privilege

Professional promotion in rank and pay is almost automatic by seniority. Positions of responsibility and authority, that is, power, are relatively few, however, and these are reserved for the ablest in a given year group. Only these stay in the company beyond the customary retirement age of 55 as the company's highest officials. The relatively early retirement age in itself somewhat protects the company from seniority-promoted officials coasting.

Strategic corporations do try to limit permanent employment to the core of operatives their ongoing revenues will support. Much of the corporation's work, especially at the lower levels, is done by noncareer personnel. Much of the work force in factory and office is young women who retire when they marry or married women who return as part-time workers. Much of the strategic corporation's factory work is done by subcontractors who often do not provide permanent employment. Moreover, much of a corporation's work may be done by temporary, noncareer workers hired as individuals at low pay (half the career man's pay) for three months to a year. Temporaries reached a peak of 12 percent of the large factory work force in 1960, though in some circumstances, almost all an industry's new hires may be temporaries, and they may make up a third or more of a given industry's work force.[22]

Permanent positions are so generous to those who hold them that survival of the institution requires that they be limited in number. There are instructive parallels to this in vocationalized educational and military institutions in the West. There is a great gap in the treatment of tenured faculty and nontenured instructors at most U.S. universities, for example, with much of the work at lower levels in fact being done by the latter. The military reserves many tasks for low-bid contractors because of the prohibitively high cost of using uniformed career personnel for its most mundane tasks.

Unlimited Professional Opportunity

Directors do constitute a privileged group in the world of the strategic corporation. They enjoy only comparatively modest advantages of wealth (since they are never given personal property in the company) but enjoy very great advantages in terms of authority and power. Every entering professional employee has a fair opportunity, an identical opportunity, of reaching the very highest posts in the corporation. All of the senior managers, namely department heads and the president, who collectively also constitute the board of directors, are recruited internally from among the larger body of the corporation's professional employees. (The exception, of course, is that in satellite companies and public policy companies, a director or two, sometimes a president, may be appointed by the senior corporation or agency.) They are co-opted. That is, new directors, and the president, are appointed by the old directors already sitting. However, new directors are selected only from among the most senior employees on a basis of ability and service. All professional employees are eligible. Moreover, the directors' elections usually reflect the consensus that emerges among the senior employee's own year group.

Promotion is automatic by seniority up to the mandatory retirement age of 55. Only a very few outstanding employees are selected as department heads and directors to stay on beyond this cutoff point. They then enjoy enormous authority. Employees approaching 55 normally have served together for 30 years, by which time a consensus has almost always emerged as to who the most able and deserving members of their group are. It is normally those so regarded whom directors recruit into their own number; others in the year group retire.

Japanese workers may value resourceful service, integrity, brilliance, and so on for their own sake. But Japanese professional employees can also fairly assume that these qualities may bring them into a position of personal authority over millions in corporate assets. Corporate service may bring to any one of them positions of great power and prestige in their society. Moreover, all persons who are not professional employees of the corporation are excluded. Professionals within the company are rewarded with a monopoly on these coveted posts. This enhances the hopefulness and loyalty of all of them throughout their careers, not just the few who are eventually chosen. This arrangement also may enhance the prestige and influence of all these employees all the time in the greater society: Any one of them could become the corporation's president or a director.

In this feature, as in so many others, professional employees of the strategic corporations resemble military officers. Any officer can be a general. No non-officer can be. This is important to the loyalty and prestige of the whole corps. Generals, once appointed, are rewarded with great responsibility and prestige and comfortable salaries, but not personal property in the institution. In all this the professional employee of a strategic corporation and the modern military officer are much alike.

Technical Employees

The technical employees of strategic corporations, like the professional employees, enjoy remarkable advantages. They also are recruited on a basis of character, educational achievement, and general promise, not for particular skills. They are recruited only upon graduation from high school, not in mid-career. Like the professional employees, they are encouraged to feel an elite consciousness based on education. The best corporations hire professionals from the best universities and workers from the best high schools. Second-line corporations hire from second-line universities and high schools. Japanese higher schools follow the pattern of the European gymnasium, which means they provide the equivalent of one or two years of college education in the U.S. system. Many higher-school graduates have studied calculus and six years of English. Even though not university-bound, they have other opportunities in the society, and strategic corporations go to great lengths to recruit and retain the best people from this zone of the society.[23]

Like the professional employees, the technical employees are guaranteed permanent employment and automatic promotion in rank and pay based on seniority. In other words, they are assured not only of career security but of career success. Like professional employees, they enjoy a wide range of fringe benefits: company housing; family allowances; inexpensive health insurance; free classes in languages, flower arranging, and such; organized sports activities; and the rest.[24]

In spite of all this, permanent employment is voluntarily abandoned by technical employees at a much greater rate than by professional employees. Apparently, a third to a half of the high school graduates hired by strategic corporations for permanent technical positions choose to separate by their twelfth year. Numbers for voluntary separations for professional employees are much smaller, on the order of 10 percent over their whole careers. The reason is perhaps that the talented technical employees see better opportunities outside the factory, for example, running their own businesses or the family farm. This in itself may explain some of the company's solicitude.[25]

Supervisors and other professional employees, when in the technical employees' environment, wear the same company uniforms, eat in the same dining halls, and belong to the same company union that the workers do. The object is to raise the self-esteem and morale of the technical work force rather than alienating workers needlessly.

There is a democratic element in treatment of the technical work force. Technical employees, like professional employees, are invited to participate, not in all decisions but in decisions on matters they know about and care about. For workers this means mainly decisions about the shop floor and plant. Workers are routinely consulted on policies affecting working conditions, on improvement in production techniques, on matters of workshop discipline, on improvement of safety, and on improvement of welfare facilities. Work force suggestions are not only widely solicited, they are widely submitted and widely implemented. Shop-floor democracy has the advantage of raising worker morale and keeps workers from feeling alienated in their own workplace. It has the further advantage that workshop decisions are made by people who are well informed and interested, not by someone in the home office who may be barely informed. In other words, this system may produce better decisions.[26]

About a third of the workers' pay, and for that matter also of the professional workers' pay and the president's and directors' pay, is in the form of bonuses. Bonuses are given out twice a year, in an amount of about one-sixth the worker's pay each time. This accustoms workers to saving a third of their pay. The bonus may be regarded as a form of large-scale structured savings. It also functions to encourage workers to identify their own well-being with that of the performance of the company. It encourages them to help their colleagues even if these co-workers are outside the department or even when co-workers face an unusual problem that the person helping has no formal responsibility for. This is because the bonus is an identical proportion of pay for everyone, in all departments, from the president down to the youngest recruit. It is a collective incentive that encourages a collective identity and the individual's devotion to the whole. Workers identify with the prosperity of the whole because that prosperity comes directly back to them.

The worker's bonus varies directly with the company's performance. In a good year bonuses can approach 50 percent of remuneration. Exceptional revenues are never distributed outside the company. The part of exceptional revenues that is not retained is always distributed to every worker in identical shares, routinely and automatically. Profit-sharing in this form is widespread among workers in strategic corporations. Workers have a stake in their company in the very concrete sense that its performance directly affects their pay from month to month. This animates them.[27]

What are we to make of the strategic corporation's technical work force? It is worth noting in this connection that workers sing the company anthem and do exercises together in the morning, wear crisply pressed uniforms and company badges at all times, and are encouraged to feel personal loyalty to the company.[28] All this is in addition to the permanent employment, seniority promotion, an early-retirement pattern, control over the workplace, company housing, comprehensive health care, family allowances, recreational opportunities, and the like. No work force in a comparable Western institution has these many remarkable features unless one considers the military to be a comparable institution. In that case, almost all of these extraordinary features become suddenly familiar and, indeed, taken for granted and insisted upon. Strategic workers are tantamount to a non-commissioned officer corps. Uniforms? Anthems? Personal loyalty? Impossibility of switching institution? Shared dress and mess in the workplace? Seniority promotion? Company housing? Family allowances? Health care? Solicitude about recreation? Difficulty retaining the best people? It is all there. Strategic workers are treated very much like a modern noncommissioned officer corps.[29]

Unions: Formalizing Labor Conflict

Strategic unions in Japan differ from conventional trade unions in the West. The difference is that strategic unions' purpose is to accommodate workers' interests, tangible and intangible, and thereby keep workers' morale and incentive high and so enhance, or at least not unduly obstruct, production. Strategic unions reduce the costs of labor conflict in large part by formalizing it, that is ritualizing it. Conventional unions' purpose, in the United States and England, often seems rather simpler: to transfer as much wealth as possible from the company to workers by threatening and conducting substantial strikes, not ritual ones.

The strategic union is supposed to keep the workers' enthusiasm and disposition to serve high in a way that does not disturb their company's ongoing production, financial health, or harmonious relations with management. Strategic management for its part is supposed to automatically devote part of revenue increases to its workers' payroll and the rest to expanding capacity. As a practical matter, rewarding workers for service and enhancing production are fairly compatible goals. Management is also supposed to look after worker morale by respecting the workers' elected representatives, heeding their suggestions whenever possible, and supporting union activities, sporting events, and such that build morale. The union has some of the same objectives as the company's personnel department, and in some areas, the union and the personnel department work closely together.[30]

Labor relations in the strategic corporation are vestigial and stylized. They are like a morality play where the players know their parts—the community also knows the players' parts—and the happy ending is known in advance to everyone. The scenario is that each March, company management offers a modest pay increase; union leaders reject this proposal as inadequate and schedule a strike of one or two days duration, always timed to coincide with good April weather. Management, faced with this overwhelming gesture, offers a little more, which the union leaders now accept, followed by general self-congratulation all around. This same pattern of conduct, the same gestures with the same results, has been almost universal among strategic corporations since the first "spring struggle" was organized by the Sohyo federation of unions in 1955.[31]

Why do they go through all this? If management is already committed to providence and solicitude toward workers, why is the ritualistic union activity necessary? The reason probably is that without the adversarial rituals to regularly prod them and remind them, management might soon forget to be provident and solicitous. Power by its nature lapses into presumption, and subordination by its nature lapses into resentment. The ritual of workers united in revolt against management, and the ritual of isolated management acquiescing to their demands, is apparently a drama needed to combat these tendencies of overt presumption above and covert resentment below. These tendencies, if allowed to grow, could jeopardize the performance of the strategic corporation. They are constantly present, and so is union activity.

There may be more to this still. It may be that the act of revolt itself is refreshing and necessary for the worker not to feel claustrophobic in the otherwise hyperdisciplined environment of the company. James C. Scott refers to the first act of rebellion by a subordinated people as "Saturnalia." One does not usually think of modern labor relations as a Saturnalia of ritual revolt. But there may be an element of this in Japanese labor relations. An act of self-affirmation by a subordinate may be satisfying in itself, quite apart from tedious questions of pay. The proverbial contentedness of Japanese workers may derive in part from their having a few days of ritual rebellion programmed in every spring and getting it out of their systems.[32]

However, labor harmony achieved through low-cost rituals is what happpens only when this system works. If either side perceives the other as acting in an immoderate, selfish way that is incompatible with the interests of the whole institution, the ritual struggle can degenerate into a real struggle. This kind of strike, a "real" strike, is rare in postwar strategic corporations. Such strikes did take place from time to time, however, in the prewar and immediate postwar years.[33] They exist in the shared memory of both sides, and both sides know the possible price if the rituals fail, which may be why the rituals widely succeed.

The function of strategic unions is in a sense analogous to that of strategic cartels. The cartels allow constructive competition among corporations but prevent obstructive competition. Unions do something like this in relations between workers and management. The purpose of the unions is, at as little cost as possible, to secure a fair share of the fruits of increased productivity for the worker and to secure for management freedom from strikes and other forms of obstruction. Historically it works. Wages have gone steadily up, and production days lost to strikes are proverbially few.[34]

The structure of strategic unions parallels that of strategic industry. Each corporation has its own in-house union, which in many corporations seems to have the status almost of a department of the company. Young professional employees are assigned as union administrators. These work with councils of union representatives who are elected from the shop floor. All employees, professional and technical, belong, up to, but not including, the section chief. It is the corporation's union that calls strikes and bargains.[35]

The unions of corporations in a given line of production band together to form a common federation, for example, a federation of electrical workers or of metal workers. This level of organization corresponds to that of the industrial association for the industry. The common federations do not negotiate, but they coordinate pay demands and strikes among the corporation member unions. The common federations for each industry in turn usually belong to a national labor confederation whose purpose is lobbying the opposition parties for labor causes at the National Diet level, both to provide legislation favorable to labor and to make sure the climate of public opinion is favorable to labor. This activity is balanced, of course, by Nikkeiren, the federation of industrial employers, which lobbies mainly the management-oriented Liberal Democratic Party (LDP).[36]

Strategic unions are deliberately fashioned entities. They are practically a department of the company and are run by administraters who are on the company payroll or tantamount to it. However, much as banks and passthrough public policy companies mimic the market, the deliberately fashioned unions mimic natural unions. They negotiate for wages and bonuses with management. They insist on managers' respect for workers in matters large and small. They lobby management for better working conditions. They carry on a variety of activities to enrich workers' lives, such as fielding company softball teams or putting on arts and crafts exhibitions, sometimes with the assistance of the company's personnel department. Moreover, as we have seen, the union orchestrates the vestigial spring strikes.[37]

In sum, the unions exist to buoy up worker morale by empowering workers to implement what the public has come to view as a fair distribution of wealth between the worker and the corporation, namely that some but not all of increased revenues will be shared each year with workers at every level (the rest of the increase being devoted to expanding or improving production), all by a cost-efficient ritual struggle, not a costly substantive struggle.

A key to all this functioning smoothly, however, may be the environment of continuous industrial expansion. The real wages of workers have doubled again and again since the war.[38] Workers and their elected union representatives alike have come to believe, perhaps with some reason, that what is good for the corporation is good for them. Some observers are convinced that Japan's economic growth is due to social peace, but the opposite dynamic may be the more powerful one. Social peace, and the remarkable harmony of the Japanese union system, may be possible because of the pervasive pattern of ever-expanding wages and job opportunites. Social peace may depend on growth, not vice versa.

The Factory as Laboratory

In the West, design functions and production functions are often separated. Engineers and laborers rarely meet. Workers may be as passive with respect to productivity goals as the machines they tend. They are merely told what mechanical act to perform, and they do it. One problem that may result is that workers may soon become indifferent or worse. Another problem is that the only persons who are really in a position to understand and expedite the factory production process, the workers, have no role in efforts to improve it.

In Japan's strategic economy many factories have been transformed into experimental laboratories whose purpose is to develop and perfect the production process. Such factories function as laboratories and are called laboratories.[39] In the case of the Toshiba corporation, for example, there are two kinds of factory, the "development factory," which perfects the design of product and process, and the "mass production" factory, which is set up only much later when the production process is perfected. The numerical majority of Japanese factories are apparently of the development type. At Toyo Denki Kaisha (TDK), one of the firms supplying Toshiba and perhaps not untypical, 60 percent of the 3,500 employees are engineers and only 10 percent are line workers.[40] The engineers work closely with the assembly-line workers in their efforts to simultaneously raise quality and quantity and lower costs.

The engineers' most important job is not to design the product, which is relatively simple, but to design the process for making the product perfectly, cheaply, and in very large volume. To do so, they must experiment long and patiently not only with the product but with the assembly line. This means working on the line themselves in close touch with the line workers. Workers' suggestions are strongly promoted.[41] There is normally a counterpoint between production design and process design. Often the product must be changed to achieve a process goal, making it easier to assemble, for example, or easier to test for defects. There is no divorce of work force from technology in these factories. The workers themselves, being mainly engineers, develop the process technology.

Designing perfect factories, not just perfect products, has dramatic results. Between 1972 and 1980, the time required to assemble a Japanese color television set fell from six hours to one and a half hours. At the same time, the number of defects was greatly reduced. This was achieved by reducing the number of components in a set, by increasing automation of component insertion, by reducing the number of circuit boards in a set, and by configuring components to allow automation of testing for defects. In other words, this miraculous result was achieved by contrapuntal redesign of product and process by engineers elbow to elbow with workers on the factory floor.[42]

Only when product and process have been perfected are "mass production" factories opened in which the production system is fixed and does not change and in which most of the production workers are high school graduates, not engineers. Such factories thus from the beginning produce high-quality, high-quantity, low-cost goods. The specialization into development factories and mass production factories is widespread. At Toshiba, the development factory is called the Manufacture Engineering Laboratory; at NEC, the Production Engineering Development Group; and at Hitachi, the Production Engineering Research Laboratory.[43]

The Japanese manufacturing company is a kind of engineers' paradise. Engineers rub shoulders with workers in the factory and rub shoulders with the customers in their company's retail shops. The purpose is to allow them to constantly redesign product and process to meet the end users' real needs. Moreover, engineers in manufacturing corporations are much more influential in management and more often become corporation presidents than in Western companies. This may be because Japanese corporations do not need financing and marketing strategies. Government plans and coordination automatically provide financing and markets. This allows the manufacturing corporation to focus all its innovative powers on manufacturing. Such companies are led, therefore, by creative engineers, not by creative accountants.[44]

Satellite Companies

There are about 200 strategic corporations, the 187 members of the neo-zaibatsu presidents' clubs plus a few independent large-scale exporters such as Toyota and Toshiba. These 200 premier companies are close to government policy and have the attributes of strategic corporations set out earlier: autonomous management, lifetime employment, seniority promotion, and the rest. These 200 companies are at the bottom of the pyramid of authority that runs from MITI through the neo-zaibatsu and the industrial associations.

At the same time, each of these companies is at the top of its own pyramid of smaller satellite companies. Each strategic corporation has from 10 to 200 smaller corporations in its system. The 187 neo-zaibatsu corporations together control some 8,476 affiliated client corporations, meaning they own between 10 and 100 percent of each affiliate's stock. On average, there are 45 companies under each neo-zaibatsu corporation. Usually the client corporations are arrayed in hierarchical tiers. Toshiba, for example, has 200 companies in its first tier and 600 in its second tier.[45]

These client firms are often called subcontractors. They exist to supply parts to the strategic corporations. The second tier, sub-subcontractors, provides parts for the parts. Automakers are noted for having the most elaborate of these supplier pyramids. To acquire 1,500 parts for an automobile, Toyota relies on four tiers of parts suppliers. The 170 companies in the first tier provide already-assembled major components; for example, Nippon Denso furnishes electronic gear. Below this are three more tiers, each providing progressively more minor components to the one above. Each tier tends to have more companies, each with fewer employees, than the one above. The lowest of the four tiers has several thousand companies, often with only a few employees each. At this level, the firm's only relation to Toyota may be that it sometimes sells to it. In Toyota's case, most of these lesser companies are also geographically clustered within a 20-mile radius of Toyota City near Nagoya.[46]

Companies in the first tier of affiliates may have all or some of the attributes of strategic corporations. Companies in the second and lower tiers may have some or none of those attributes. These often tiny lower-level firms sell to strategic corporations but are not strategic corporations. They have a relationship to strategic corporations somewhat analogous to that of a small civilian contractor's relationship to the military. It is perhaps fair to describe the strategic economy as confined to the 200 strategic corporations proper and their approximately 10,000 affiliated clients. Moreover, even these 10,000 satellite firms may experience the effects of strategic economy only to a degree.

The dynamics of coordination that operate between the strategic corporations and their subordinate tiers of suppliers are similar to those that operate in the authority chain that runs from MITI through the neo-zaibatsu to the strategic corporations. There is multilevel planning. In other words, each level reveals its plan to the lower and guarantees markets, capital, and technology. Each lower level, wishing to benefit from these guarantees, strikes a plan compatible with the level above. In other words, the system follows principles of noncoercive incentives to achieve plan conformity. It relies heavily on positive inducements in the form of market opportunities, funds, and access to new technology. Discipline in these lower levels, as above, is accomplished through competitive pluralism. Toyota buys each part from several different suppliers, obliging them to compete on quality and price.

Major manufacturing in Japan is more structurally compartmented than in the West. Major Western corporations tend to do their own manufacturing of components and to pursue several lines of business, often unrelated, thus reducing risk. Japanese manufacturing corporations tend to make only one product and at only one level of assembly, which, however, increases risk. The Japanese manufacturing company's scope of activity is narrower than that of most Western companies, allowing it to focus intently on that business and to be held responsible for it by the echelon above. What the West does with one large company, the Japanese do with a cluster of small companies hierarchically arrayed and with complex ongoing inter-corporation relationships.

This approach has some functional advantages, but also some unnecessary complexities. It is to some extent an idiosyncratic artifact of the social modularity of Japanese culture, not a consequence of the intrinsic logic of production. Japan tends to "groupism," meaning not only that individuals tend to aggregate into groups but also that large groups tend to disaggregate into smaller ones. If strategic economy were ever adopted in another cultural milieu, it might not manifest this extremely compartmented quality.

Nonstrategic Companies

Only a few of Japan's corporations are strategic corporations. Japan has approximately 1.7 million incorporated firms, of which only about 200 are full-fledged strategic corporations. Some 10,000 more are affiliated client companies in the strategic system. All the rest of Japan's million corporations, including even some in the lowermost tiers of suppliers to the strategic system, are not strategic corporations. Nonstrategic corporations come in all sizes but tend on the whole to be smaller and have lower wages. They may have some of the same features as strategic corporations, or they may have none. They may have influential individual investors, a president who makes many times what his employees make, hierarchical supervision, and nonguaranteed employment.[47] In other words, they may have the qualities one might usually expect of a small commercial organization rather than a large strategic organization. Nonstrategic corporations belong to the Japan Chamber of Commerce and Industry, not to the Federation of Economic Organizations (Keidanren), which is the national federation of the strategic corporations.[48]

Corporate Destiny

Strategic corporations and their satellites are largely protected by the system from obstructionist conduct by each other and from idiosyncratic changes in market and financial conditions. But they are not protected from their own failures. A corporation that consistently performs less well than its competitors may lose orders and funding—and go bankrupt. The further down the corporation hierarchy one goes, the more exposure there is to this result. Japanese company employees feel they are "on the same side in a commercial war" on whose outcome their collective livelihood depends. Success means immediate enrichment for everyone in the company through the bonus system. Failure means collective hardship.[49]

The Japanese corporation and everyone in it has a shared destiny. This makes employees' lives more interesting. There is an element of adventure in a career if there is something at stake, exhilarating especially if there is the possibility of enrichment and empowerment through one's own outstanding efforts. What makes human beings happy is not to be free of adversity but to face adversity, or opportunity, and prevail. Happiness requires an optimum degree of adversity. It is not a favor to a work force to shelter it entirely from the consequences of its performance. The lack of institutional destiny seems to have plagued the Soviet industrial experiment.

The Strategic Corporation: What Is It?

The strategic corporation viewed functionally is not exactly what we think of as a private enterprise. It may be more useful to think of it as a sophisticated, modern public institution. External ownership is part of the system but as a practical matter it is unenfranchised. The corporation's employees are collectively self-governing and enjoy an exceptional degree of empowerment and prestige. All this appears to foster in them a vocationalized loyalty such that they are able to apply large amounts of public capital to public policy goals, doubling production, for example, without a major portion of that wealth being diverted to nonstrategic purposes.

How shall we compare Japanese strategic corporations to U.S. strategic corporations? We cannot do so easily because the United States has no corporations that are quite like this. Japanese strategic corporations are "Japanese" in the sense that they are structured such that, to prosper, they must serve the policy interests of the Japanese people and, of course, the policy interests of their own institutional health. The United States does not appear to have any companies that are structured in quite this way. Nonetheless, some understanding of Japan's strategic corporations can be achieved provided we are willing to draw comparisons to some of the United States' well-established public institutions as well as to its private commercial ones.

Notes

1. For several scholars' observations to this effect, see Ronald Dore, *British Factory–Japanese Factory* (Berkeley, CA: University of California Press, 1973), pp. 275–76; and Clyde V. Prestowitz, *Trading Places* (New York: Basic Books, 1988), p. 156.

2. Cf. Alexander K. Young, *The Sogo Shosha: Japan's Multinational Trading Companies* (Boulder, CO: Westview Press, 1979), p. 55; Douglas M. Kenrick, *The Success of Competitive Communism in Japan* (London: Macmillan, 1988), pp. 5, 6.

3. Dore, *Factory*, pp. 164–65; and see *Corporate Disclosure in Japan: Reporting*, The Japanese Institute of Certified Public Accountants ed. (Tokyo: JICPA, 1984), pp. 18–19, 84–85.

4. See Michael Gerlach, "Twilight of the *Keiretsu*? A Critical Assessment," *Journal of Japanese Studies* 18:1 (Win 92): 79–118, p. 92; Michael Gerlach, "*Keiretsu* Organization in the Japanese Economy," pp. 141-74 in Chalmers Johnson, Laura D'Andrea Tyson, and John Zysman eds., *Politics and Productivity* (New York: Ballinger, 1989), pp. 156–62.

5. See Gerlach, "*Keiretsu* Organization," pp. 168–69.

6. Ibid., p. 157; Young, p. 55; Richard E. Caves and Masu Uekusa, "Industrial Organization," pp. 459–523 in Hugh Patrick and Henry Rosovsky eds., *Asia's New Giant* (Washington, DC: Brookings Institution, 1976), p. 467.

7. See, for example, Caves and Uekusa, p. 467; and Tadanori Nishiyama, "The Structure of Managerial Control: Who Owns and Controls Japanese Businesses?" pp. 123–63 in Kazuo Sato and Yasuo Hoshino eds., *The Anatomy of Japanese Business* (Armonk, NY: M. E. Sharpe, 1984), pp. 123–24, 132–33.

8. Young, p. 51; Caves and Uekusa, p. 467.

9. Gerlach, "*Keiretsu* Organization," p. 157, has a good discussion of stockholding defining neo-zaibatsu relations. The direct quote is from Rodney Clark, *The Japanese Company* (New Haven: Yale University Press, 1979), p. 86, cited by Gerlach, ibid. Clark, p. 86, also discusses the stockholding issue.

10. See, for example, Charles J. McMillan, *The Japanese Industrial System* (Berlin: Walter de Gruyter, 1984), p. 291, for Sumitomo Bank's takeover of failing Mazda in the late 1970s; and Gerlach, "*Keiretsu* Organization," pp. 153–54 for Mitsubishi Bank's takeover of failing Akai Electric in the early 1980s.

11. See Young, p. 55; Caves and Uekusa, p. 467; James C. Abegglen and George Stalk, *Kaisha* (New York: Basic Books, 1985), p. 185; Eleanor M. Hadley, *Antitrust in Japan* (Princeton, NJ: Princeton University Press, 1970), p. 251.

12. Clark, pp. 125–26.

13. See Abegglen and Stalk, p. 192. In 1991, 407 U.S. corporation presidents received $1 million or more in pay and benefits, according to Reuters' "Executive Pay Hits New Highs," *New York Times*, May 11, 1992, p. C5.

14. Prestowitz, pp. 153–54; James C. Abegglen, *Management and Worker* (Tokyo: Sophia University, 1973), p. 24.

15. Abegglen, p. 62; Dore, *Factory,* pp. 98–102.

16. Abegglen, pp. 101–02, 184–86; Clark, pp. 198, 200; Prestowitz, p. 156.

17. See, for example, Prestowitz, p. 156; Kenrick, p. 5; Nishiyama, pp. 123, 133.

18. Clark, p. 126; Dore, *Factory,* pp. 227–28.

19. Clark, p. 129; Dore, *Factory,* p. 227.

20. Clark, p. 130.

21. Ibid., p. 133.

22. Ibid., p. 174; Andrew Gordon, *The Evolution of Labor Relations in Japan* (Cambridge, MA: Harvard Council on East Asian Studies, 1985), p. 401.

23. Abegglen, pp. 76, 179, 181; Ronald Dore, *Taking Japan Seriously: A Confucian Perspective on Leading Economic Issues* (Stanford: Stanford University Press, 1987), p. 206. For possible origins of elite labor consciousness based on education, see George O. Totten, "The Great Noda Strike of 1927–1928," pp. 398–436 in Bernard S. Silberman et al. eds., *Japan in Crisis* (Princeton: Princeton University Press, 1974), p. 421.

24. Abegglen, pp. 101–02, 184–86.

25. See Gordon, pp. 396–99 for separation figures. See Thomas P. Rohlen, *For Harmony and Strength* (Berkeley, CA: University of California Press, 1974), pp. 83–84, for a discussion of other reasons employees resign.

26. Dore, *Factory,* p. 166. McMillan, p. 167.

27. Dore, *Factory,* p. 108; Abegglen, pp. 29, 36, 183; Rohlen, p. 164.

28. See, for example, Rohlen, pp. 34–43 on anthems and entrance and other ceremonies as developing company loyalty.

29. I have argued elsewhere that there is also an early-modern cultural influence, the tradition of the *sotsu* samurai, that helps explain the society's perceptions of the elite technical work force. There were two tiers of samurai in Tokugawa Japan: *shi,* professional servants of the feudal lord, his administrators, scholars, and such; and *sotsu,* foot soldiers who guarded the lord's person, trained his falcons, minded his palace, and the like. The latter, the *sotsu* class of samurai, were often highly skilled, did all the lord's physical work, and were expected to have a deep emotional loyalty rather than a loyalty rooted in philosophical study. If the *shi,* professional samurai, provide a kind of modal historical identity for the "salaryman," it may not be too far off the mark to assume that *sotsu,* the foot soldiers, do the same for Japan's technical work force. See Thomas M. Huber, "Men of High Purpose," pp. 107–27 in Tetsuo Najita and J. Victor Koschmann eds., *Conflict in Modern Japanese History* (Princeton, NJ: Princeton University Press, 1982), pp. 125, 126. See also Thomas C. Smith's insightful and persuasive *Native Sources of Japanese Industrialization, 1750–1920* (Berkeley, CA: University of California Press, 1988), "Peasant Time and Factory Time in Japan," pp. 199–235, for influences on the modern Japanese work force deriving from Japanese village life. For another interesting perspective on these issues, see also W. Mark Fruin, "Instead of Management: Internal Contracting and the Genesis of Modern Labor Relations," pp. 109–134 in Tsunehiko Yui et al. eds., *Japanese Management in Historical Perspective* (Tokyo: University of Tokyo Press, 1989).

30. Rohlen, pp. 186–87.

31. Dore, *Factory,* pp. 176–78; Gordon, pp. 382–83; Robert E. Cole, *Japanese Blue Collar* (Berkeley, CA: University of California Press, 1971), p. 226.

32. James C. Scott, *Domination and the Arts of Resistance* (New Haven, CT: Yale University Press, 1990), p. 202.

33. For one of the substantial prewar strikes, see Totten. For a brief discussion of a postwar strike at Hitachi, see Dore, *Factory*, pp. 117–18. For a discussion of labor relations in the period 1945–1953, see Gordon, pp. 329–74.

34. Manufacturing wages in Japan grew by a factor of 20 times, 2,000 percent, in real terms between 1953 and 1987, according to *Japan Statistical Yearbook*, Statistics Bureau ed. (Tokyo: Japan Statistical Association, 1988), p. 785. In recent years, Japan's 1.7 million firms have experienced 2,000–4,000 strikes per year, over 80 percent for less than half a day's duration. See ibid., Table 3-44, "Labor Disputes by Kind," p. 115.

35. For company employees as union administrators, see, for example, Rohlen, p. 184.

36. Dore, *Factory*, pp. 121, 124–25; McMillan, p. 183; Gordon, pp. 372, 375–76; Cole, pp. 225–27.

37. Rohlen, pp. 184, 186–87; Dore, *Factory*, pp. 163–75.

38. See note 34.

39. Christopher Freeman, *Technology Policy and Economic Performance: Lessons from Japan*. London: Pinter, 1987, pp. 41, 45.

40. W. Mark Fruin, lecture, University of Kansas, Lawrence, April 11, 1990.

41. McMillan, p. 167.

42. Ira C. Magaziner and Thomas M. Hout, *Japanese Industrial Policy* (Berkeley, CA: Institute of International Studies, 1980), pp. 27–28.

43. Freeman, p. 45.

44. McMillan, pp. 166, 167, 236.

45. Young, p. 38; Gerlach, "Twilight," p. 88; T. J. Pempel, "Japanese Foreign Economic Policy: The Domestic Bases for International Behavior," pp. 723–74 in Peter J. Katzenstein ed., *Between Power and Plenty: Foreign Economic Policies of Advanced Industrial Countries*, published as a special edition of *International Organization* 31.4 (Aut 77): 581–920 (whole volume), p. 734.

46. For Toyota geographical clustering, see Kiyoji Murata and Isamu Ota eds., *An Industrial Geography of Japan* (London: Bell and Hyman, 1980), pp. 158–60.

47. Some of the differences between "modern" and "traditional" firms are listed in Dore, *Factory*, p. 302. For the 1.7 million figure, see Gerlach, "*Keiretsu* Organization," p. 145.

48. McMillan, pp. 57–59.

49. The quote is from Clark, p. 199. Clark, pp. 199–200, discusses the relative precariousness of Japanese companies.

PART TWO

INTERNATIONAL STRATEGY

5
Global Presence: Structures of Implementation

WE HAVE SEEN that certain sectors of Japan's domestic economy are shaped in their broad outline by the will of the Japanese public and are shaped in their particular manifestations by vocationalized public officials in the government who are serving that will. These sectors are rationalized, structured, and planned to meet certain of the society's needs: constantly growing wealth, constantly rising incomes, constantly improving products and capacity, constantly rising rewards for education and ambition, social harmony, and so on. These sectors of Japan's economy at home are "strategic" in the general sense that officials coordinate resources on a large scale, in a reactive and intelligent way, for particular policy ends.

Certain institutional features of Japan's economic presence abroad are "strategic" in this sense but also in a narrower conventional sense: They promote Japan's economic interests in the international arena and are so configured that they may under some circumstances do so adversarially against other nations' corporations or political interest groups. These institutional elements of Japan's economic presence abroad have an ensemble of attributes that may allow them to function as an instrument of policy, somewhat analogously to a modern diplomatic service or military service. Although the military analogy obviously will not take us too far here, a brief reflection on the usefulness of a modern military establishment may be an aid in this instance to understanding some of the advantages inherent in maintaining a strategic-economic presence abroad. Military assets, whether or not in active use, may serve as an important lever for promoting the interests of a modern state. Credible military force, by its very existence, may have a pervasive influence on both friends and foes, persuading them to assume certain courses of action. Edward Luttwak has called this powerful effect "suasion." It is safe to say that suasion is the main purpose of modern military force and that such force need not usually be used except to adjust credibility. The same is true of strategically deployable economic assets. They exercise a powerful suasion. Dominant resources in the area of goods, technology, and capital, by their very existence, may have a pervasive influence on the conduct of other nations. Such resources constitute international suasion or influence.[1]

The Japanese economy is a policy economy in both dimensions. It serves domestic policy and foreign policy. The object of domestic economic policy, simply put, is to provide constantly improving access to a rewarding life and livelihood for everyone in the society. The object of foreign economic policy, naturally enough, is to achieve influence in the international environment. Rapid, planned production expansion serves both of these goals. It is advantageous for both dimensions of policy, domestic and international. Small wonder there is an enduring political consensus behind it.

The dominance of the twin policy considerations in the organization and operation of the Japanese economy helps explain what may be that economy's central paradox: The Japanese economy produces but does not consume. A major proportion of production in strategically important consumer categories—autos, electronics, optics, machine tools, semiconductors—is exported, not domestically consumed. Per capita industrial production is among the highest in the world, on par with Sweden's or Switzerland's. Yet per capita consumption remains behind that of most of Western Europe and North America. Japan is first in production but far from first in consumption. Why?

What possible purpose could modern production have if not to accommodate consumption? It is a question serious students of Japan must ask because Japanese government policy does simultaneously both expand production and restrain consumption, exporting the difference. Japan's strategic economy first serves international strategic and domestic social goals; it serves goals of individual consumption only incidentally and secondarily. It provides every Japanese with a good job and a good life and provides Japan the nation with influence. It does not necessarily provide every Japanese with state-of-the-art consumer goods ad libitum.

In practice, the economy does eventually provide citizens with state-of-the-art cars and cameras and such, but only when and to the extent that doing so is compatible with larger policy goals. Small-retail consumption is a low priority in the Japanese system, and less is granted later in this sector because consumption is not itself the primary object. The average citizen's experience, despite brisk production levels, is material austerity. He has a good production job but with somewhat restricted access to the products. In Japan, domestic consumption is restrained in order to achieve rapid expansion of techno-industrial wealth for international strategic goals, but also to achieve the overriding domestic goals of prosperity and expanding vocational opportunity.

Organization: MITI

Evidence is growing in the works of serious Western analysts that in their purpose, organization, and dynamics, certain Japanese economic operations in the international arena are strategic in nature rather than commercial. In other words, they entail coordinating a number of agencies for a policy purpose, not merely conducting market transactions for cash gain. The entity that is usually viewed as overseeing this kind of work is, of course, the Ministry of International Trade and Industry. The implementation system for international trade is largely analogous to that for domestic industry. Coordination in both spheres is exercised by the same agency to ensure compatibility. Fashioning policy on an ongoing basis is MITI's International Trade Policy Bureau (see Table 2.1). Converting policy into usable plans and supervising implementation at the highest level is MITI's International Trade Administration Bureau. It is extremely advantageous for export and import policy to be closely coordinated with domestic production policy. Therefore a single umbrella ministry, MITI, oversees both domestic "Industry" and "International Trade."

The International Trade Policy Bureau includes the Office of International Trade Policy Planning, the International Trade Research Office, the Overseas Public Affairs Office, the U.S.-Oceania Division, the Oceania–Latin American Office, the West Europe–Africa–Middle East Division, the Middle East–Africa Office, the South Asia–East Europe Division, the North Asia Division, the Economic Cooperation Division, the Technology Cooperation Division, and more.[2]

The International Trade Administration Bureau includes the Trade and Foreign Exchange Affairs Office, the Standards and Certification Office, the Inspection and Design Policy Office, the Export Division, the Import Division, the International Trade Insurance Division, and more.[3]

MITI's control of international trade is grounded in customary practice, of course, but also in certain key statutes. The most fundamental of these is the Foreign Exchange and Trade Control Law. The Trade Control Law gives MITI comprehensive powers to control major movements of funds and goods across Japan's borders. One of the law's essential control mechanisms is that MITI approval is required for payments of funds on a commercial scale to interests outside the country. This provision in itself represents a major empowerment. It gives MITI authority to constrain or facilitate international economic transactions, in the service of policy needs. Nonpolicy imports are constrained because currency cannot move abroad to pay for them. Nonpolicy exports are constrained because

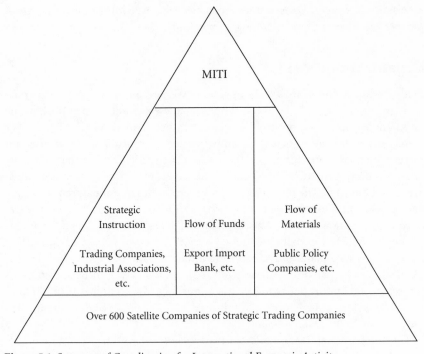

Figure 5.1 *Structure of Coordination for International Economic Activity*

nonconforming exporters might soon find that they could not obtain permission to pay for imported raw materials. In practice, this power is usually used to oblige manufacturers to export finished products and to constrain the import of manufactured goods. The Trade Control Law is administered jointly by the International Trade Administration Bureau, the Industrial Policy Bureau (domestic), and the Ministry of Finance. The law was apparently diluted somewhat in 1979.[4]

Specific tariffs and quotas are perhaps superfluous in Japan because historically at least the Trade Control Law in and of itself has given MITI a blanket quota authority over goods and funds moving internationally. If importing something is outside MITI's policy intent, such action is unlikely to be approved, and indeed it may be unwise for a would-be nonconformist importer to annoy MITI by making the request. Tariffs are rigid and ineffective by comparison to this permissions procedure. Tariffs are a perhaps outmoded tool for shielding domestic industries compared to the constant intelligent adjustment that has been, or at least for a short while was, possible under the Trade Control Law.

Even so, there are many other statutory empowerments for control of trade besides the Trade Control Law. MITI's International Trade Administration Bureau has jurisdiction as well over the Export and Import Transactions Law, the Export Inspection Law, the Export Goods Design Law, the International Trade Insurance Law, and others.[5]

Three Methods of International Implementation

MITI uses three means to orchestrate domestic economic activity: direct instruction, coordination of flows of capital, and coordination of flows of materials. It uses these same three methods to influence international economic activity. For each of these avenues, MITI relies on a constellation of mediating institutions, as it does for the domestic economy (see Figure 5.1). In the realm of direct instruction, MITI can mobilize general trading companies, one-product trading companies, export councils, and industrial associations and cartels. For distributing capital, MITI can utilize the Export Import Bank of Japan, the Overseas Economic Cooperation Fund, and the 12 city banks. To determine movement of materials, MITI can employ public policy companies; the Foreign Exchange and Trade Control and other transactions laws; and tariffs, quotas, and taxes administered by itself and the MOF.

General Trading Companies

Just as MITI relies on neo-zaibatsu and industrial associations to respond to instructions in the area of domestic strategy, it relies on trading companies to develop its strategies abroad (see Figure 5.2). Just as the neo-zaibatsu represent a remarkable concentration of resources, so do Japan's famous general trading companies.

Not surprisingly, the trading companies are in close and continuous contact with MITI officials. They are virtually unique institutions in the world of global trade. There are a dozen multiproduct trading companies in Sweden, Canada, and elsewhere, but they are far smaller than their Japanese counterparts. In comparative scale of operations, the Japanese companies are truly colossal. Every one of Japan's 10 general trading companies has annual sales larger than the total trade of many countries. As of 1982, they had $350 billion in sales, $90 billion more than the top 10 U.S. multinational corporations combined. In 1976, the 10 major companies handled 18 percent of Japan's domestic commerce. They handled 56 percent of all Japan's imports and 56 percent of all its exports. This amounted to 5.3 percent of all the world's international trade.[6]

We have seen that in the domestic economy, Japanese planners prefer to have 6 to 10 enterprises engaged in any given activity in order to ensure pluralist fluidity and competitive discipline. To this end they maintain six omnicompetent supercombines, the neo-zaibatsu. It is not too surprising, then, to find that Japan has 10 giant multiproduct, multiservice trading companies, the so-called "general

Figure 5.2 *Vertical Coordination Pattern for International Trade*
SOURCE: Derived from *Tsusan handobukku [MITI Handbook]*. MITI Handbook Editing Committee ed. Tokyo: Shokokaikan, 1989, pp. 35–64; Alexander K. Young, *The Sogo Shosha: Japan's Multinational Trading Companies*. Boulder, CO: Westview Press, 1979, pp. 37, 46; T.J. Pempel, "Japanese Foreign Economic Policy: The Domestic Bases for International Behavior." Pp. 723–74 in Peter Katzenstein ed., *Between Power and Plenty: Foreign Economic Policies of Advanced Industrial Countries*, published as a special edition of *International Organization* 31.4 (Aut 77), p. 750.

trading companies," and that the largest 6 companies of these 10 happen to be leading members of their respective neo-zaibatsu groups (see Table 5.1). The remaining 4, somewhat smaller, also have close neo-zaibatsu ties, though (as with the 6 non-neo-zaibatsu city banks, for example), these ties are not as exclusive as for the member six.[7]

Just as MITI combines domestic and foreign strategy operations in one agency for coordination purposes, so does each neo-zaibatsu. In this respect as in others,

Table 5.1 *Japan's 10 General Trading Companies and Their Major Neo-Zaibatsu Affiliations*

Company	Neo-Zaibatsu
Mitsubishi Corporation	Mitsubishi
Mitsui and Company	Mitsui
Sumitomo Shoji	Sumitomo
Marubeni Corporation	Fuyo
C. Itoh and Company	Daiichi
Nissho-Iwai Company	Sanwa
Toyomenka	Mitsui et al.
Kanematsu Gosho	Daiichi et al.
Nichimen	Sanwa et al.
Ataka and Company	Sumitomo et al.

SOURCE: Based on Young, Alexander K. *The Sogo Shosha: Japan's Multinational Trading Companies.* Boulder, CO: Westview Press, 1979, pp. 26, 43; Yoshihara, Kunio. *Sogo Shosha: The Vanguard of the Japanese Economy.* New York: Oxford University Press, 1982, pp. 306–11.

the neo-zaibatsu functions as a mini-MITI. In other words, the big six general trading companies are the overseas representatives both of Japan, Incorporated and of their respective neo-zaibatsu. Three diamonds, the mark of the Mitsubishi group, may be seen around the world on products as diverse as canned fruit and huge tracked power shovels. This is not a market accident. It is a consequence of the global presence of Mitsubishi Corporation, the Mitsubishi group's overseas action arm.

The big six trading companies are not externally owned in the conventional sense but rather are part of the crossholding pattern of stock ownership that characterizes neo-zaibatsu corporations in general. As with other neo-zaibatsu members, interownership may be thought of as resembling collective self-ownership, such that management is in practical terms largely autonomous except, of course, for ties of responsibility to MITI and to other neo-zaibatsu members. In other words, it is the "top executives, middle-level managers, and other employees of the trading companies ... who ... control Japan's ten largest *sogo shosha* [general trading companies]."[8]

Like other neo-zaibatsu members, the big six are a conduit for publicly controlled bank funds to their client firms, mostly producers in Japan and potential purchasers overseas. Funds move from BOJ to the city banks to the trading companies, and then to hundreds of client companies. All neo-zaibatsu corporations lend capital to client corporations, but the trading companies do so on a larger scale. They function somewhat like city banks specializing in international rather than domestic trade. Access to city bank funds gives them financial leverage in transactions around the world, to open a giant copper mine in Africa, for example, or to sell on credit a turnkey petrochemicals plant in southeast Asia. The trading companies also lend to hundreds of small export-related businesses in Japan, however. The advantage of this is that the trading companies can assess the merit of these known small firms far better than can city banks, who themselves have no ongoing business with the small firms.[9]

One consequence of the major trading companies being a conduit for public capital is that they are highly leveraged. They practice "overborrowing," as do other strategic nonfinancial corporations, but to a greater degree such that typically their liabilities are equal to 97 percent of their assets. In other words, their global credit business, as a conduit of funds, is so large that they have net assets of only 3 percent of their gross capital. This peculiarity is interesting also in light of the fact that these giant corporations make almost no profit. The 10 general trading companies did $350 billion of business as of 1982 but netted less than one-fourth of 1 percent of this amount as profit.[10]

What, then, is the purpose of these large, intensely competitive companies that, however, have no net assets and take no profits? The answer may be that they are not commercial companies in the conventional sense. Rather they appear to be strategic institutions that exist primarily to implement Japanese national policy in the area of international commerce. Wealth transfer to themselves, except at the level of maintenance, may not be their object. Their object instead is apparently to orchestrate global patterns of trade in a manner favorable to Japan.

Various observers report that the general trading companies gather strategic information on a global scale. The trading companies gather strategic data of every imaginable sort about foreign nations: tactics of competitors; attitudes of government officials, labor, and consumers; credit standing of distributors; political trends; price movements; recent technical advances; and even the weather.[11]

The scale of this data-gathering activity is remarkable. Marubeni has 130 telex stations around the world passing 20,000 messages a day to its Tokyo headquarters. Another trading company's communications center in Tokyo occupies an entire floor, thousands of square feet filled with telex, facsimile, and computer terminals linked to 187 offices in 77 countries. Still another has 11 exclusive computer-linked telephone lines to New York, and 6 to London. Despite the considerable costs of this activity, this information is disseminated promptly and at almost no cost to client firms and to MITI.[12]

Strictly speaking, the 10 trading companies may not be commercial companies in the conventional sense. Instead they appear to be Japan's influential quasi-private trading agencies abroad, the overseas representatives of Japan's techno-industrial policy interests.

Satellite Corporations

The big six general trading companies control some 600 client firms. Each of the six owns controlling interest, 10 percent or more of outstanding stock, about 100 subordinated affiliates. Mitsubishi Corporation has 94 such firms; Mitsui and Company, 135; Sumitomo Shoji, 73; Marubeni Corporation (Fuyo), 115; C. Itoh (Daiichi), 121; Nissho-Iwai (Sanwa), 78.[13]

About two-thirds of these 600 satellite corporations are located in Japan and one-third are located abroad. About half are in commercial services: sales, distribution, transportation. About one-third are in numerous manufacturing industries. The client corporations depend on the big six for raw materials, for sales abroad, and for capital.[14]

As is the case for other neo-zaibatsu member strategic corporations, each of the big six represents an institutional constellation of as many as 100 corporations.

Global Presence

The six neo-zaibatsu trading companies maintain a nearly global presence. As of 1980 Japanese trading companies of all types employed 30,000 Japanese around the world, most of them apparently corporation officers, not support personnel. The 10 major general trading companies alone maintained 908 overseas offices.[15] General trading companies' presence in the United States is illustrative. The 10 companies operate 100 headquarters and branch offices in the United States, employing 1,500 officers from parent companies. The headquarters offices, that is, the U.S. affiliates, have gross assets of up to $1 billion and "are all located at the ... most prestigious sites in midtown New York." They handle 85 percent of U.S. exports to Japan and 50 percent of imports from Japan to the United States (most of the rest being handled by the one-product trading companies of Toyota, Matsushita, and the like). Each of the big six neo-zaibatsu-affiliated general trading companies handles 1 to 2 percent of all U.S. exports in a given year.[16]

Japan's 10 general trading companies, the overseas representatives of Japan, Incorporated, maintain hundreds of offices and tens of thousands of officers around the globe. Global trading systems are not new. They have been a feature of world affairs continuously since the Portuguese set up the first global trading empire in the sixteenth century.[17] Still, in terms of pervasive coordinated control over both information flows and real events, there is probably no global trading system in modern history that is quite the equal of postwar Japan's.

Other Trading Companies

The general trading companies handle acquisition abroad of foodstuffs, raw materials, and semifinished materials, usually in vast quantities, from around the world. They also sell semifinished commodities such as steel, cloth, and semiconductors, also in large quantities, around the world. They sell producers' goods to industries abroad and turnkey plants, resource development projects and various construction projects to industries and governments abroad. They do a great deal else by way of conducting information and technology back to Japan and handling various sorts of political coordination in foreign countries.[18]

It is for doing this broad variety of things all around the world that these companies are called "general trading companies." Still, there are several things the great trading companies do not do. They do not handle machinery and appliances destined for the retail consumer abroad, and they do not handle the export abroad of small-scale or highly specialized production items. In other words, general trading companies handle mainly large-scale transactions.

Consumer electronic and optical goods, and autos, sold one by one around the world, albeit in millions of items, are handled by trading affiliates of the giant one-product production groups in electronics and autos—Toyota, Nissan, Honda, Matsushita, Sanyo, Sharp, Toshiba, Sony, and the rest—and are not handled by the general trading companies. The reason seems to be that these industrial groups are, as it were, specialized one-product zaibatsu in themselves and operate outside the sphere of the neo-zaibatsu groups. They therefore tend not to rely on the neo-zaibatsu-affiliated trading companies for their sales. They do not require general trading company brokerage because the sale is to individual consumers, not to the corporations or governments that are the great trading companies' usual clientele. Instead they must reach millions of individual consumers with brand recognition, sales outlets, and the like. Moreover, the electronic goods and autos need specific kinds of servicing after sale for the individual customer, and the giant trading companies normally neither sell nor service on a small retail scale.[19]

A third category of trading company besides the general trading companies and the one-product-for-consumers trading companies is the so-called specialized trading company. These sell abroad light industrial products such as toys and umbrellas or specialized products such as hospital supplies made in southern Japan for Asian markets. They often sell only a specialized particular product to a specialized geographic area and so are small in scale compared to the general trading companies or to the high-technology, high-volume global market auto and electronic trading companies. As of 1973, Young counted 9,743 of these small, specialized firms engaged in foreign trade.[20] They are the analog of the numerous small-scale, low-technology, low-wage quotidian industries in Japan itself. They have limited strategic impact, and MITI does not bother to exert much control over them except, of course, to prevent their importing unauthorized manufactures into Japan or exporting strategic raw materials from it.

The world of the trading companies mirrors the world of domestic industry. General trading companies operate abroad for the domestic neo-zaibatsu. High-technology, global-production volume trading companies handling autos and electronic goods operate on behalf of the one-product domestic zaibatsu such as Toyota. Thousands of smaller firms operate abroad on behalf of the domestic economy's nonstrategic mundane zone, firms that lie outside the privileged strategic world of the neo-zaibatsu yet are still obliged to act compatibly with it.

Export Councils

Besides being able to communicate international economic policies to domestic corporations through general and one-product trading companies, MITI can convey them through export councils. In the domestic economy MITI works through neo-zaibatsu but also through industrial associations and cartels. Industrial associations and cartels themselves are in many cases export-oriented. Where such organizations are insufficient, MITI has established export councils. In 1954, almost immediately after the U.S. occupation ended, Japan set up an Export Council consisting of the prime minister, other relevant ministers, the director of the Bank of Japan, and business leaders. It met regularly to explore methods of expanding exports and to set export goals. Its function evidently was to coordinate activities between MITI and other ministries. Its current version is the Japan Foreign Trade Council, whose daily administration is operated by MITI's International Trade Administration Bureau.[21]

Also established in 1954 were separate export councils for a number of industries, the equivalent of the industrial associations in the domestic economy. These, too, still do a thriving business. They are affiliated with the International Trade Administration Bureau and include the Japan Chemical Exporters Association, the Japan Machinery Exporters Association, the Japan Iron and Steel Exporters Association, and so on.[22] Some industries heavily oriented to export, such as autos and electronics, seem not to have their own exporters' associations, suggesting that their domestic industrial associations themselves are perhaps being used as the main agency of export policy.

The export councils' function is evidently to communicate export policy to the industries that carry it out and also to coordinate these industries' activity so as to eliminate obstructive competition while preserving policy-achieving competition, much as industrial associations routinely do for domestic industry. Export councils are one of the institutional means, like the general trading companies and the one-product trading companies, that MITI uses to provide direct instruction on export matters to implementing industries.

Import councils exist as well under MITI's sway and also answer to the International Trade Administration Bureau. The united council is the Japan Federation of Importers Associations. They include the Japan Chemical Importers Association, the Japan Sugar Import and Export Council, the Japan Lumber Importers

Association, and others.[23] Here also, important categories of raw materials are missing, such as iron ore, bauxite, and petroleum, suggesting that import policy for many items is handled through domestic industrial associations, general trading companies' import divisions, and public policy companies and not always through import councils. That is, the import councils may be organized only for certain imported commodities that are not already effectively coordinated through other institutional agencies.

Orchestration of the Flow of Funds: The Export Import Bank

As in the domestic economy, MITI influences trade outcomes by exercising policy regulation over flows of money. International financing dynamics are also closely analogous to their domestic counterparts. Setting the pace here, in place of the Bank of Japan, is the Export Import Bank of Japan (EIBJ). Just as the BOJ opens major reservoirs of publicly controlled savings to domestic manufacturers for strategic production goals, the EIBJ draws on part of these same funds to implement strategic policy abroad.

The EIBJ is, unlike the BOJ, a subordinate agency of MITI's International Trade Administration Bureau. It has its main office in Tokyo, a branch in Osaka, and 15 representative offices around the world. The EIBJ's capital as of 1985 stood at about $7.7 billion (967 billion yen). EIBJ also held as part of its lendable funds about $38 billion (4.8 trillion yen). These funds were lent to EIBJ by other government accounts, namely the General Account and several other accounts; most of the latter's assets flow originally from the Postal Savings System. Of course, these $38 billion are merely pilot funds. The 12 city banks are expected to participate by combining with the EIBJ to make joint loans or else to lend their own funds for the same projects, much as BOJ obliges the city banks to do to expand domestic manufacturing. This augments the effect of the $38 billion loan fund by greatly increasing the available capital.[24]

The EIBJ has three basic functions, all of which amount to providing abundant ready capital to nourish Japan's strategic goals abroad: domestic lending, direct loans, and liability guarantees. Domestic lending, in turn, has three purposes. The first is to finance the export of equipment produced in Japan and the technological preparation the purchasing country needs to use the equipment. Second, domestic lending expedites the import of raw materials crucial for the export strategy. Third, domestic lending supports Japanese corporations launching investments or enterprises abroad.[25]

Direct loans by the EIBJ are made to foreign governments, banks, and corporations. They are of four types, the first being loans tied to the import of equipment from Japan. The second is loans of industrial or import funds not explicitly tied to particular transactions with Japan. The third is loans to foreign interests for capitalization of joint ventures with Japanese firms. Fourth is refinancing, meaning to supply funds to foreign governments who would otherwise default on their obligations to Japanese corporations because of balance-of-payments problems, for example.[26] Direct loans are ostensibly made to foreign interests, but most of these funds seem to end up in the hands of Japanese firms nonetheless.[27]

The Export Import Bank carries on a third major category of transaction, liability guarantees. These, of course, support the pilot-lending pattern. They amount to guarantees on the funds provided by the 12 city banks for a wide variety of trade-related projects the EIBJ supports. The EIBJ guarantees funds lent jointly by the city banks and itself. It also guarantees domestic loans by city banks that parallel EIBJ domestic loans. Since 1985 the EIBJ has also guaranteed direct loans made by city banks to foreign institutions.[28] The principle at work here is to expedite city bank lending, especially to export manufacturers, by reducing the risk for the banks.

In addition to depending on the Export Import Bank, Japanese strategists rely on the Overseas Economic Cooperation Fund (OECF). The OECF was set up in 1961 under MITI's International Trade Policy Bureau in response to expectations of world public opinion that Japan should play a more active role in world development. The OECF was evidently an upgraded version of the Southeast Asia Development Cooperation Fund, which had existed earlier under the jurisdiction of the EIBJ. OECF capital was inherited from the Southeast Asia Development Cooperation Fund, which was capitalized originally from the General Account and which had also accumulated profits from its own transactions.[29]

OECF loans in principle serve the development of industry in Southeast Asia and other areas. Its loans are for development projects, development research, economic stabilization, and capitalization. Development-project lending is to support industries in developing countries "that will promote economic exchange with Japan." Preparatory development research by or in a foreign country is also funded by OECF loans. OECF lends also for "stabilization:" It provides funds to import materials needed for a country's economic stability. Finally, OECF occasionally grants funds, instead of lending them, for capitalization. This means, apparently, that the OECF may make funds available to a developing country wishing to acquire a Japanese-built plant when the country cannot afford it even with easy credit. In practice, OECF developmental lending overlaps with the direct foreign lending by the EIBJ, which is ostensibly for trade promotion. This overlap evidently continues despite reforms of 1975 meant to reduce it. Most OECF funding, like EIBJ direct foreign loans, seems to end up in the hands of Japanese firms pursuing strategy-compatible goals.[30]

Orchestration of Flows of Materials: Public Policy Companies

Besides instructing general trading companies and export councils in policies it favors and determining flows of money, MITI regulates the movement of materials by giving general mandates to certain quasi-autonomous, monopoly-status agencies designed specifically to do only this. In other words, the flow of certain materials is governed quasi-autonomously by public policy companies as well as through MITI directives to trading companies, import councils, and industrial associations. These materials include foodstuffs such as meat and sugar and recreational substances such as alcohol and tobacco. What amounts to import monopolies are created for these commodities. Monopoly status permits public policy companies to purchase abroad in very large amounts, giving them a monopsony leverage that may sometimes allow them to buy below world market prices.[31]

Monopoly status also allows PPCs to resell in Japan at prices far above world market prices. Such PPCs, moreover, may serve to nearly eliminate foreign competition for domestic producers of certain goods even when, and perhaps because, these producers are relatively inefficient, as in the case, for example, of beef producers. The considerable profits from these transactions are drawn off and placed in government-controlled capital funds, from which they may make their way to subsidizing favored domestic manufacturers and exports. Sometimes the profits may go directly from the public policy company to the subsidized industry, as in the case of sugar monopoly proceeds being handed over for a number of years to the then rapidly growing shipbuilding industry.[32] These agencies answer to MITI or to other ministries that coordinate their activities with MITI. They work smoothly in part because they use market-conforming methods. They emulate the conduct of private monopoly traders to generate market leverage and profit.

The public policy companies that monopolize the import of sugar, meat, and the like are quasi-autonomous passthrough companies. Their main raison d'être is to serve as valves regulating the flow of these materials in accordance with ministerial policy. Many other institutions, industrial associations, industrial cartels, and import councils sometimes may be used to govern the flow, price, and distribution of imported and exported materials. This is not, however, their sole function, as is the case with structures such as the sugar monopoly. Tax policy also may sometimes be used to coax materials in the direction of policy needs. Duties on imported raw materials may be forgiven, or extraordinary depreciation rates allowed, for the manufacture of goods that are exported. This simple tax practice creates a financial incentive for materials to flow toward strategic production and away from nonstrategic production.[33]

As in the domestic economy, regulation of the flow of materials is one of the three principal devices at planners' disposal. This device is of less relative importance than in the domestic economy, however, because it is effective only at the gate, that is, at the boundary between the Japanese economy and other nations' economies. Postwar planners are not in a position to establish legal monopolies over the flow of materials in foreign countries. In foreign contexts MITI officials must rely more on direct-instruction structures such as the general trading companies, since they lack the option of public policy monopolies that they enjoy at home.

Prospero's universe abroad, the constellation of structures on which economic planners can rely to implement policy goals, embraces some institutional elements not found in the domestic system, such as the general trading companies and the OECF. Still, the same basic approaches are employed: policy instruction, orchestration of the flow of funds, and orchestration of the flow of materials.

Coordination with Other Policy Levers

Statesmen and stateswomen in most nations today have at their disposal three institutional systems that are structured so as to be responsive to policy ends: diplomatic systems, military systems, and intelligence systems. Statesmen, moreover, may influence, for policy ends, cultural and commercial and other assets that are not structurally responsible to national authority.[34] This is the case in today's Anglo-American environment. In Japan, certain major techno-industrial assets appear to have been removed from the second category, one of influence, to the first category, of structured responsibility. U.S. statesmen are at pains to closely coordinate diplomatic, military, and intelligence activity for national policy objectives. Which zone has priority and which is secondary depends on the actual political situation at a given moment. Priority is given to the area where most is at stake, now diplomacy, now military, and so on. Japanese statesmen appear to coordinate these three policy instruments with Japan's international industrial policies. Indeed, Japan is viewed by some as having given nearly continuous priority to promoting national industrial policies, subordinating other diplomatic, military, and intelligence policy to the goals of techno-industrial expansion. Japanese statesmen may sometimes give priority to economic policy on the same basis that Anglo-American statesmen sometimes give priority to military policy: That happens to be the institutional system by which, under currently existing circumstances, they feel the nation can achieve a decisive advantage or avoid a decisive disadvantage. When at war most nations give military objectives priority because in that circumstance, military outcomes have the greatest impact on national interests. In peace, Japanese statesmen at times appear to give industrial expansion a similar priority, and for the same reason. That is the area that may most enhance or attenuate national interests in real existing circumstances.

Prospero's universe is the globe. MITI organization mirrors the geographical and political configuration of the world, as a perusal of the divisions of the International Trade Policy Bureau will show.[35] Perhaps not surprisingly, MITI posts its young officials early in their careers not only to each of Japan's prefectures but also to embassies and consulates around the world or else to one of the overseas offices of Japan's techno-industrial intelligence service, the Japan External Trade Organization (JETRO).[36] Let us consider JETRO further.

Strategic-Economic Intelligence: JETRO

Japanese statesmen carry on strategic intelligence gathering with the purpose of achieving industrial policy objectives. The intelligence service they rely on is the Japan External Trade Organization. In fact, Japan has a full complement of intelligence organizations for acquiring diplomatic intelligence, military intelligence, domestic national security intelligence, and so on. In addition to this usual quiver of intelligence organizations, however, Japan seeks out information tailored to the needs of economic strategy. The agency that does this work, JETRO, is highly developed, perhaps to make up the difference in an environment where Japan's military intelligence organizations are comparatively small. JETRO tends to gather general strategic information and not only techno-industrial information.[37]

JETRO was established by legislation of the Japanese National Diet on April 26, 1958. From that time it has been fully funded, fully staffed, and fully controlled by MITI. It is perhaps the most prominent agency supervised by MITI's International Trade Administration Bureau. JETRO's nominal existence began far more modestly, however, as a trade promotion group organized by the mayor and some industrialists in Osaka in 1954. MITI took a prompt interest and by 1955 was infusing 100 million yen per year from the national banana import monopoly. With the legislation of 1958, however, MITI was able to freely appoint its own officers and use general account funds in operating JETRO.[38]

JETRO is a "world wide intelligence service," or an "international commercial intelligence service" that exists to convey "economic and political intelligence ... to Tokyo."[39] It is likely that JETRO specializes in higher level strategic intelligence such as the likely future conduct of foreign governments and that the 10 general trading companies specialize in operational and tactical intelligence, for example, where soybeans might be bought or where machine tools might be sold. MITI officials ultimately have access to both categories of information, of course. JETRO as of 1975 maintained 24 trade centers and 54 offices in 55 countries. By 1984 there were over 100 such establishments.[40]

In the United States, for example, MITI operates eight JETRO offices, in New York, San Francisco, Chicago, Los Angeles, Houston, Atlanta, Denver, and Puerto Rico. JETRO was obliged in 1969, albeit after 11 years of operation, to register as a foreign agent by the U.S. Justice Department. Apparently JETRO then set up the United States–Japan Trade Council as an unregistered surrogate organization. The U.S. Justice Department sued, noting that 90 percent of the Trade Council's funds came from the New York mission station of JETRO. The Trade Council thus also was obliged to file as a foreign agent in 1976.[41]

MITI may rely on JETRO for several other purposes besides intelligence reporting. MITI, apparently through diplomatic attachés and JETRO officers, coordinates and supervises Japanese companies' patent infringement, dumping, or other legal disputes abroad. This allows MITI to apply more resources than the isolated company could and to coordinate action at the political level, relying on lobbyists and various pro-Japanese constituencies, and at the judicial level, obtaining reliable lawyers. JETRO also maintains a science watch, scanning technical developments in foreign countries.[42]

Strategic policies require strategic information and effective data gathering requires a well-developed global intelligence service: JETRO. Needless to say, international techno-industrial strategies are closely coordinated with international informational activities, and this is most probably facilitated by their being overseen by the same agency, MITI's International Trade Administration Bureau.[43]

International Strategy

Japan's strategic economy operates in two different dimensions, one domestic and the other international. It is really two discreet systems with different objectives and plans that have to be coordinated. Even so, methods of implementation in the two systems are fairly analogous: strategic instruction, coordination of funds, and coordination of materials.

There is accumulating evidence in the scholarship of serious Western observers that certain aspects of the international dimension of Japanese economic activity are strategic in nature, not commercial, and that they respond to public policy priorities rather than merely to market conditions. This likelihood is strongly suggested by the highly structured quality of many aspects of Japanese economic activity abroad.

Notes

1. See Edward N. Luttwak, *Strategy: The Logic of War and Peace* (Cambridge, MA: Belknap Press, 1987), pp. 190–95; cf. also Carl Von Clausewitz, *On War*, Michael Howard and Peter Paret trans. (Princeton, NJ: Princeton University Press, 1984 [1833]), p. 87.

2. *Tsusan handobukku* [*MITI Handbook*], Tsusan handobukku henshu iinkai ed. [MITI Handbook Editing Committee ed.] (Tokyo: Shokokaikan, 1989) [hereafter *MITI Handbook*], pp. 35–47.

3. Ibid., pp. 48–64.

4. For the text of the law, see *Tsusho sangyo roppo* [*International Trade and Industry Laws*], Tsusho sangyo-sho ed. [MITI ed.] (Tokyo: Marui Kobunsha, 1988) [hereafter *MITI*

Laws], pp. 3–16. For a translation of the law, see Robert S. Ozaki, *The Control of Imports and Foreign Capital in Japan* (New York: Praeger, 1972), pp. 143–62. For jurisdictional responsibility over the law, see *MITI Handbook*, p. 526. For changes of 1979 see Chalmers Johnson, *MITI and the Japanese Miracle* (Stanford, CA: Stanford University Press, 1982), pp. 302–03.

5. For the International Trade Administration Bureau's jurisdiction, see *MITI Handbook*, p. 526. For these and other trade-related laws, see *MITI Laws*, pp. 3–203.

6. Charles J. McMillan, *The Japanese Industrial System* (Berlin: Walter de Gruyter, 1984), p. 237; Alexander K. Young, *The Sogo Shosha: Japan's Multinational Trading Companies* (Boulder, CO: Westview Press, 1979), pp. 4, 17–18, 50, 195, 197; T. J. Pempel, "Japanese Foreign Economic Policy: The Domestic Bases for International Behavior," pp. 723–74 in Peter J. Katzenstein ed., *Between Power and Plenty: Foreign Economic Policies of Advanced Industrial Countries*, published as a special edition of *International Organization* 31.4 (Aut 77): 581–920 (whole volume), p. 750.

7. Young, pp. 26, 43; Kunio Yoshihara, *Sogo Shosha: The Vanguard of the Japanese Economy* (New York: Oxford University Press, 1982), pp. 306–11.

8. Young, pp. 51–55.

9. Ibid., 58; Yoshihara, p. 217.

10. Young, pp. 72, 74; McMillan, pp. 237–38.

11. McMillan, p. 234; Young, p. 61.

12. McMillan, p. 234; Young, p. 67; Yoshihara, p. 219.

13. Young, p. 46.

14. Ibid.

15. Ibid.; McMillan, p. 239.

16. Young, pp. 204, 208–10.

17. See Charles R. Boxer, *The Portuguese Seaborne Empire, 1415–1825* (London: Hutchinson, 1969), and Sanjay Subrahmanyam, *The Portuguese Empire in Asia 1500–1700: A Political and Economic History* (London: Longmans, 1992).

18. McMillan, pp. 233, 240; Young, pp. 208–09.

19. McMillan, p. 239.

20. McMillan, p. 238; Young, p. 13.

21. Pempel, p. 750; Young, p. 129; *MITI Handbook*, p. 629.

22. Young, p. 129; *MITI Handbook*, pp. 634–43.

23. *MITI Handbook*, pp. 643–49.

24. Ibid., p. 627; Yoshio Suzuki ed., *Japan's Financial System* (Oxford: Oxford University Press, 1987), pp. 292–93.

25. Suzuki, p. 293.

26. Ibid.

27. On these dynamics, see Christopher Freeman, *Technology Policy and Economic Performance: Lessons from Japan* (London: Pinter, 1987), p. 43; Pempel, pp. 750–51.

28. Suzuki, p. 293.

29. *MITI Handbook*, p. 587; Suzuki, p. 294.

30. Suzuki, p. 295.

31. See, for example, Chalmers Johnson, *Japan's Public Policy Companies* (Washington, DC: American Enterprise Institute, 1978), pp. 29, 45, 49, 152, 159, 163. Also cf. Leon Hollerman, *Japan's Economic Strategy in Brazil* (Lexington, MA: Lexington-Heath, 1988), p. 228, on large purchases leveraging low prices.

32. Tuvia Blumenthal, "The Japanese Shipbuilding Industry," pp. 129-60 in Hugh Patrick ed., *Japanese Industrialization and Its Social Consequences* (Berkeley, CA: University of California Press, 1976), p. 144.

33. Joseph A. Pechman, "Taxation," pp. 317–82 in Hugh Patrick and Henry Rosovsky eds., *Asia's New Giant* (Washington, DC: Brookings Institution, 1976), p. 357; Ira C. Magaziner and Thomas M. Hout, *Japanese Industrial Policy* (Berkeley, CA: Institute of International Studies, 1980), pp. 51–52; Pempel, p. 749.

34. Cf. e.g. Luttwak, pp. 179.

35. Cf. *MITI Handbook*, pp. 39–42.

36. Johnson, *MITI*, p. 62.

37. On the various Japanese intelligence services, see Jeffrey T. Richelson, *Foreign Intelligence Organizations* (Cambridge, MA: Ballinger, 1988), pp. 249–265.

38. Johnson, *MITI*, pp. 231–32; Johnson, *Policy Companies*, p. 13; *MITI Handbook*, pp. 626–27.

39. P. B. Stone, quoted in Johnson, *Policy Companies*, p. 51; Johnson, *MITI*, p. 230; Pat Choate, *Agents of Influence* (New York: Alfred A. Knopf, 1990), pp. 140–41.

40. Johnson, *MITI*, p. 231; McMillan, p. 104.

41. Johnson, *MITI*, pp. 231–32; Choate, pp. 140–41.

42. Clyde V. Prestowitz, *Trading Places* (New York: Basic Books, 1988), p. 261; McMillan, p. 104.

43. *MITI Handbook*, pp. 626–27. Note, however, that other economically active ministries besides MITI also influence and are served by JETRO. JETRO holds five directors' seats open to outside agencies, of which MITI controls two, Agriculture one, and Foreign Ministry one. The fifth seat is negotiated between MITI and other ministries. See Johnson, *Policy Companies*, p. 112.

6

Strategic Objectives:
Tending the Gate and
Operations Abroad

WE HAVE EXPLORED the institutional structure of Japan's strategic economy abroad and the potential of that structure to function as an instrument of international policy, rather as a modern diplomatic, military, or intelligence service might do. We can now address more closely the question of objectives: What are the elaborate international economic structures meant to accomplish? Later we will be able to consider how some of these objectives are implemented domestically, at the portal between Japan and the world, and abroad.

Most commentators today assume that there are several distinct levels of strategy in the domain of military security. Edward Luttwak argues that there are five: grand strategy, theater strategy, operational strategy, tactical strategy, and technical strategy.[1] We will not go too far wrong if we assume that in a global conflict such as World War II, there were five or so levels of strategic policy for globally operating powers such as the United States or Britain. These would include (1) the political strategy, meaning the nation's international political goals and the plans needed to achieve them; (2) the global military strategy, meaning the military goals and plans believed necessary for implementing the global political goals; (3) the theater strategy, meaning the goals that had to be attained in each theater to accomplish the global military goals; (4) the operational strategy, namely the goals that had to be realized by constituent corps, divisions, and regiments within theater to achieve the theater goals; and (5) the tactical strategy, meaning the goals of battalion-sized and smaller units necessary to bring about the divisional and corps objectives. Each strategic level in World War II had its own distinctive attributes, institutional structures, dynamics, and objectives.

It is probably fair to say that Japan's global strategic economy has six or so strategic levels: (1) international political; (2) global economic; (3) regional and zonal economic (the equivalent of "theater"); (4) task-group economic, meaning the action of particular supervising bureaus, neo-zaibatsu, industrial associations, cartels, or other groups of corporations within a geographical region (the equivalent of "operational"); (5) corporate economic, meaning the action of individual corporations within a region (also the equivalent of "operational"); and (6) departmental economic, meaning methods of manufacturing or sales employed by functioning departments within these corporations (the equivalent of "tactical"). Let us briefly consider Japan's strategic objectives at the uppermost levels, since they tend to be relatively neglected by Western analysts.

Political Objectives

What most ambitious world powers are reputed to strive for is perfect autonomy, freedom from any interference by other powers in their pursuits of their interests. In practice, however, this degree of freedom may require influencing the conduct of other nations in whole or in part. International influence has many levers: diplomatic, political, religious, ideological, cultural, propagandist, technical, scientific, agricultural, military, industrial, financial, transportational, and even legal and moral. Historically ambitious powers have tugged on several of these levers most of the time. Note that economic strategies can provide advantages in a number of these areas, and not just the economic ones.

Certain basic patterns of economic conduct over the last 40 years suggest that Japan may have been pursuing an economic program oriented to achieving international influence. It is rather difficult to explain much of Japan's economic conduct without reference to some intention to establish political influence over other nations. Why does Japan limit consumption to a fraction of production? Why does it restrict inflow of scarce and widely desired foodstuffs? Why does it sell products and lend funds abroad at rates less than the market rates at home? None of this enhances the material standard of living of the Japanese people. Such measures do not spring from a logic of material well-being. They can hardly be explained without reference to a logic of economic and political influence in the international arena.

Global Economic Objectives

If a measure of international influence is Japan's political objective, what does this imply, or require, in terms of its global economic strategy? What are Japan's global economic objectives? The global objectives of a strategic economy must evidently be to maximize, and constantly increase, one's strategic production and access to the factors of strategic production. Strategic production means industrial production of tradeable goods, especially high-technology, high-value-added manufactured goods, in quantities beyond what is domestically consumed so that they can easily be converted to capital flows or goods flows abroad. Production of a surplus of tradeable goods, especially high-technology tradeable goods, is of strategic value because it can easily be converted to political influence.

Factors of strategic production include capital; raw materials; a skilled technical work force; employments to sustain that work force; product and process technology; techno-industrial plant capacity itself; construction assets; transportation assets; and service assets such as insurance, marketing networks, and brokerage networks. Japan's persistent pursuit of production and factors of production, evidently in part as a means to international goals, is sometimes referred to by observers as representing a commitment by Japan to achieving "economic security."[2]

Domestic, Interface and International Zones

International economic strategy operates in three zones: domestic, foreign, and the interface between. We can begin our inquiry by first exploring relevant aspects of the domestic economy. Domestic economic operations serve two distinct sets of objectives at once: domestic social objectives and international political objectives. These two programs, domestic and international, social and political, have to some extent separate bases of political support within the Japanese public. Both agendas have to be respected. Strategic industrial systems have a positive domestic role in addition to their international role: They must provide meaningful jobs and incomes and essential consumer products for civil society. This requirement exists separately from the whole question of international aspirations.

Japan does not have one economic strategy. It has two economic strategies that are complementary: the domestic social strategy and the international political strategy. In the domestic economy, much less so abroad, these two strategies coexist and are interfused. Their complementariness is one of the most important attributes of the system in the sense that this complementariness shores up the system's political support. Strategic economy serves two purposes: social welfare and international influence. A majority of the public can always be mobilized to support one or both objectives, which may be why Japan's economic system, despite the demands it imposes, has been widely, solidly, and continuously supported at home for 40 years.

It is worth noting that even in the arena of domestic objectives, strictly economic ends are subordinated to social and political ends. Market autonomy and immediate material comfort for consumers are both set aside in favor of expanding vocational opportunities for all classes and the steady expansion of productive structures. In other words, there would be an extra-market discipline at work in the domestic economy even without the international program.

Domestic Strategy

Let us consider what is done in the domestic economy to support the international strategy. In fact we have already seen most of what is done in the domestic economy proper. By means of various mechanisms, MITI orchestrates rapid growth of strategically important production, that is, production of high-technology, high-value-added tradeable goods. Nonstrategic aspects of the economy, the quotidian economy, are by various mechanisms drawn upon to support strategic industrial activity. Consumption, both of imported raw materials and foodstuffs and of exportable manufactures, is apparently to a degree restrained, the object being to make sure that there is a surplus of manufactured goods to export and that imported materials are available for export production. In other words, the domestic economy is structured and operated so as to generate a growing surplus of high-value manufactured goods available for export. This system is explored in Chapters 1 to 4.

Interface Strategy

In a system of strategic economy, there are in effect three zones, domestic (examined earlier), foreign, and the interface between them. The interface between is the portal, the gate through which resources of all sorts pass between the domestic and foreign arenas of the system. The interface is not passive but rather determines what goods move in and out, in what quantities, by whom, and for what. Interface agencies, by controlling flows between the two systems, significantly affect events in both. The institutional structures that operate the interface are, of course, MITI and its minions: the public policy companies, the importing industrial cartels and associations, general trading companies, and large one-product trading companies. Differential taxes of various sorts levied by the Ministry of Finance and that ministry's customs service are also part of the interface system.

Japan's global strategic goals amount to acquiring production and factors of production abroad. This translates into a number of consistent policy actions in the interface zone. Interface agencies promote the inflow and inhibit the outflow of strategic production and the main factors of production: raw materials, technology, and long-term capital flows. These agencies promote the outflow but inhibit the inflow of manufactured goods. They appear to strive, moreover, to see to it that services involving movement of goods between foreign areas and the Japanese interior are placed in Japanese hands, including shipping, insurance, finance, warehousing, construction, and commercial brokerage. Let us look at some of these interface functions more closely.

Production and Export Promotion

Strategically, the assumption behind the export drive may be that by exporting, Japan is, in effect, importing production. Apparently it is some rationale such as this that underlies Japan's persistent export policy.[3] Let us consider, however, the export drive's extent and some of the means by which it is implemented. Between 1955 and 1985, the value of Japanese exports increased from 724 billion yen to 41,956 billion yen (see Figure 6.1). Almost all of this increase represented manufactured goods with increasingly sophisticated technological content. One might argue that this remarkable, persistent increase was due to an accident of the market. Most observers, however, point to a variety of governmental measures, many of them at the interface, that sustain the ever-expanding export.

The Japanese government implements international strategies using the same basic levers it uses for domestic strategy: direct instruction, regulation of funds, and regulation of materials. The direct instruction method is operated through the structures described in Chapter 5. The policies, including export promotion, are passed down through MITI to manufacturers' associations and cartels and to neo-zaibatsu trading companies. MITI might order, for example, that in one year Mitsutomo Widgets should double production, that the whole increase should be exported, attention Mitsutomo trading company, Mitsutomo bank, the widget industrial association, and so on. Direct instruction does not operate only at the interface, of course, but wherever MITI has institutional authority, at home or abroad. We have already examined in Chapters 1 through 4 how MITI goes about rapidly increasing production at home by means of direct policy instruction.

Unlike direct instruction, orchestration of funds and materials for the global strategy seems to operate at the portal, the interface, between Japan and the world because it is relatively easy to exercise regulating functions at the gate. Even the domestic strategy relies in part on orchestration of funds and materials at the interface.[4]

One method the Japanese government frequently resorts to at the interface to promote exports is a wide array of tax measures. In other words, the government provides compelling tax benefits that are conditioned on export. These include tax exemption for export revenues, accelerated depreciation, tax-free cash reserves, and numerous others. Between 1955 and 1964, the Japanese government allowed 80 percent of a firm's revenues from exports to be tax exempt.[5] Export operations, unlike other economic activity in the society, paid relatively little tax. Export industries were like ecclesiastical or educational institutions in the United States: They were doing good public works that benefitted the whole society, expanding productive employments for example, and so enjoyed major exemptions from tax. In effect, governmental services were being provided to those industries at less than cost.[6]

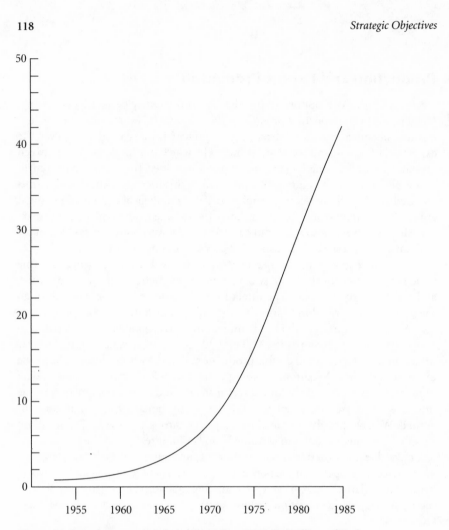

Figure 6.1 *Japan's Exports in Selected Years Since 1955 (in Trillions of Yen)*
SOURCE: *Japan Statistical Yearbook.* Statistics Bureau ed. Tokyo: Japan Statistical Association, 1988, p. 336.

This arrangement was altered in form but not substance in 1964. It developed that tax exemptions for exports were regarded by the world regulatory body, the General Agreement on Tariffs and Trade, as an unacceptable export subsidy. So the Japanese authorities replaced the tax exemption by allowing exporting indus-tries to increase their depreciation allowances on production equipment by up to 80 percent, depending on how much of their production was exported. In other words, the public financial support of exports continued at about the same mag-nitude but under a different legal rationale such that the global trade body would not object to it.[7]

This special allowance was in addition to the large accelerated depreciation deductions already allowed for many investments in strategic industrial plant. Increased initial depreciation of up to one half of acquisition cost is allowed for "important" industries. This can mean very extensive tax exemption in the first few years after investment in plant and equipment for strategic production, which much of the time is export production.[8]

Another influential tax measure besides export revenue exemptions and accelerated depreciation deductions is the tax-free cash reserve. Exporting firms are allowed to set aside part of their revenues, without their having been subjected to the corporate income tax, in cash reserves. These cash reserves may be accumulated to cover overseas losses or overseas market development, among other things.[9] There are a host of other tax measures to support strategic exports, including exemption of strategic machinery from import fees and tax deductions for royalties paid to foreign-patent holders. All of these tax measures are constantly being adjusted to meet changing strategic needs by the Tax System Deliberation Council, a senior advisory body appointed by the Minister of Finance.[10]

Tax subsidies for exports are not nominal. They are a major factor in the Japanese national budget. According to calculations by the Ministry of Finance, these amounted to $40 billion in the high-growth years 1962 to 1971. Revenue losses to the Japanese government from all special tax measures to promote industry (not including depreciation) amounted to about 10 percent of all revenues collected from corporate and personal income taxes between 1956 and 1972.[11]

Besides the major tax subsidies, which a competitive industrial corporation can hardly ignore, the Japanese government provides incentives to export in the form of insurance. In the United States, the federal government insures bank deposits, so citizens are not reluctant to put funds in banks. The Japanese government does something like this for export activity. The government thus substantially reduces export risk for strategic corporations.[12] The insurance enabling legislation, the Trade Insurance Law, is administered by MITI's International Trade Administration Bureau, which maintains a department, the International Trade Insurance Division, to implement the export insurance program.[13] The government insurance program provides for "normal" export insurance, export prices insurance, export bills insurance, export guarantee insurance, advance payment for imports insurance (evidently for raw materials), trade intermediary insurance, foreign investment insurance (to establish infrastructure in a foreign country), and "reinsurance" to reimburse other export insurers.[14]

At the same time that there are powerful direct-instruction materials flows and financial incentives to promote exports, the domestic distribution of manufactured products is constrained. There is almost no consumer credit and no tax exemption for consumer interest. The various tax and other incentives for export, such as remission of duties on imported materials, preferential freight and energy rates, and so on, often do not accrue for manufacture of products for the home market, thereby raising their prices. Moreover, there are substantial excise taxes on many high-value-added goods, which tend to limit domestic consumption further. All of this, of course, has the consequence that Japanese products sometimes cost far less in some cities abroad than they do in Japan, and that Japanese tend to travel abroad in order to shop.

Strategies of Market Access

Japan's global economic objectives amount to acquiring production and factors of production for the apparent purpose of exercising political influence. Securing a market may be viewed as tantamount to securing production. It is thus not surprising that Japanese planners employ a variety of methods to acquire markets. This practice is sometimes controversial in the eyes of statesmen of other countries because they assume that commercial relations among friendly nations in peacetime will be reciprocal. In other words, they assume a paradigm that is commercial. Japanese planners sometimes appear to be following instead a paradigm that is strategic. Their strategic interest appears to be to secure their own markets, which is relatively easy, and such other markets as may be available.[15] In other words, they seek to increase their market access as a means to achieving their global economic objective of acquiring production.[16]

There is some evidence that in securing their domestic markets, Japanese planners prefer exclusionary methods that are not conspicuous or that purport to be something other than exclusion per se. Most of these methods operate at the interface. Let us consider some of them. It is probably reasonable to assume that MITI uses direct instruction to reduce imports. It very likely makes known to industrial associations and cartels, trading companies, and public policy companies, all of which are under some degree of MITI authority, that strategic policy requires that import of manufactured goods be limited. All that may really be needed to stem many imports is to communicate that purpose to implementing agencies.

Even so, MITI relies on some formal measures in addition to direct instruction to limit imports. Importers have to be licensed, and cash deposits are required of importers. Moreover, some tariffs were historically high before foreign governments began protesting, and there have also been publicly announced quotas for some goods.[17]

In addition to direct instruction and formal barriers, MITI resourcefully utilizes several other methods. Let us consider a few of them. Sometimes goods are excluded by inspection procedures that are prohibitively elaborate and expensive. When Japanese autos needed protecting, Japanese officials imposed an inspection procedure that practically required incoming U.S. autos to be taken apart and rebuilt one by one by Japanese inspectors. The cost of this was borne by the importer, making the vehicles unsellable. Exclusion of imports was implemented in this case with a purposefully designed inspection system.[18]

Safety concerns are another rationale sometimes invoked by Japanese officials when resisting imports. For many years, foreign firms were effectively excluded from launching new cosmetics products, such as hair dyes, by a Ministry of Health and Welfare list of approved ingredients, which was kept secret.[19]

Imports are also sometimes blocked by bureaucratic or technical requirements imposed not by the government but by a strategic corporation a step or two removed in the chain of authority. The sale of optical fiber cable to Japan in the late 1970s was effectively blocked by the Nippon Telephone and Telegraph Corporation (NTT), which required at the eleventh hour that foreign suppliers use the same cable design Japanese manufacturers used, even though (or perhaps because) the Japanese design was three times more costly to produce.[20]

It is not unheard of for Japanese officials to employ several of these methods in succession, generating what might be called defense in depth. They simply deploy one technique after another until the import challenge is neutralized. Foreign-made aluminum baseball bats, for example, were excluded initially by safety standards set cooperatively by the Japanese government and the Japan rubberized baseball league. The U.S. government protested, so the Japanese government and baseball league agreed to accept any foreign bats that met the league's safety standard. The Japanese government, however, insisted on inspecting each lot of imported bats separately. The United States complained to GATT, whereupon the Japanese government abandoned its formal standard. The Japanese baseball league, however, then adapted a safety standard identical to the government's discarded one, which still effectively prevented distribution of the foreign bats.[21] In other words, Japanese officials in this case relied in succession on an exclusive safety standard, prohibitive inspection, and resistance by a regulatory institution at a lower level. They conducted a resourceful defense, a kind of defense in depth.

Japan's global economic objectives appear to require that market access be maximized. Japanese planners can be observed employing a number of methods to that end. Japan's approach to market access, unusual in today's commercial climate, can nevertheless be understood fairly easily as a manifestation of its global strategic objective of acquiring production. For this purpose Japan seems to secure its domestic markets and such other markets as may be available.

Industrial Materials

What may a strategic economy do at the interface to promote the inflow of industrial raw materials? Industrial materials are essential to production, and perpetually expanding production implies a perpetually expanding need for such materials. One of the things planners do to acquire materials is to make sure that available foreign exchange goes on a priority basis to favored strategic materials such as iron ore and coke for the steel industry. Moreover, the government provides generous long-term financing for Japanese corporations purchasing such materials. The Export Import Bank and the Overseas Economic Cooperation Fund, among other institutions, are engaged in this.[22]

Another strategy planners use for materials acquisitions is the establishment of purchasers' monopolies. The magnitude of strategic demand among Japanese corporations itself creates a serious potential problem for the system. These corporations' urgent need for supply might oblige them to bid against each other to obtain materials from foreign providers, driving up prices. This would result in disinvestment, as funds flowed through the corporations to the foreign suppliers. Such a dynamic would be disadvantageous for the system as a whole and, indeed, for each of the corporations involved. To help overcome this problem, planners tend to create purchasers' monopolies at the interface for certain industrial materials and for certain primary consumer goods. The government does not abridge the market to do this but rather emulates the time-honored commercial method of overcoming a sellers' market: monopsony.

One agency buys for all or supervises the buying for all. Doing this essential monopsony work are certain industrial cartels and associations, and public policy companies such as the tobacco and salt monopoly, the sugar monopoly, and the beef import monopoly. Similarly, the purchases of general trading companies abroad are coordinated by MITI officials so that, for example, a given foreign mine may sell its ore only to one designated Japanese trading company. This practice is sometimes called "channeling."[23]

These monopsony agencies purchase for the needs of a whole nation. This scale of demand may sometimes allow them to induce foreign providers to sell below world market prices. Japanese buyers can easily reward foreign suppliers that lower prices with large and stable orders. Monopsony purchase, and other arrangements favoring inexpensive acquisition of materials, may sometimes result in the materials' being available to Japanese companies at less than the world market price. Such companies could make a profit just by reselling the materials abroad at market price. One of the advantages of the public monopoly agency is that it can also monitor use and constrain supply to companies that try to re-export materials rather than devoting them to strategic production at home. To expedite the acquisition of industrial materials at the interface, planners make sure that the required foreign exchange is available and establish purchasing agencies to ensure that acquisition is on as favorable terms as possible.

Technology Acquisition

Technology is another one of the factors of techno-industrial production that Japanese planners are obliged by their strategic orientation to acquire abroad. Planners employ a remarkable variety of means for this purpose, both at the interface and abroad. Several of these methods suggest that the planners' frame of mind in this pursuit may be strategic rather than commercial. Basic scientific breakthroughs in the West are usually not proprietary and can be discovered simply by monitoring published and freely distributed scientific journals. Offices of general trading companies abroad routinely monitor scientific and technological discoveries around the globe.[24]

Let us explore some of the Japanese government's methods for acquiring proprietary technologies. As a practical matter, Japan in the postwar period has acquired many of its basic product and production technologies from the United States. For example, Japan obtained transistor technology from Texas Instruments and others in the 1950s, color television technology from Motorola in the 1960s, robots from Unimation in the late 1960s, optical fiber technology from Corning in the 1970s, and integrated circuits from IBM in the 1980s.[25] Much if not most of Japan's considerable engineering expertise is devoted to refining and applying basic technologies developed elsewhere.[26]

Often, Japanese corporations have merely bought the new technology at modest cost from its U.S. developers. Even this apparently cash-nexus approach, however, reflects realities that are politically shaped. The U.S. government, at least prior to the Soviet Union's collapse in 1990, encouraged U.S. firms to facilitate Japanese growth. Moreover, MITI discouraged the import of high-technology manufactured goods, so licensing the technology to a Japanese company on Japanese terms seemed the only way to profit from a technology at all in Japan. An example of Japan's acquiring a costly technology simply by buying a license is Kawasaki Heavy Industries' producing Japan's first industrial robots in 1968 under a license from Unimation, Inc.[27]

In the area of technology acquisition, as in the area of market access and a few others, Japanese planners sometimes seem to be relying on a strategic paradigm of what they are doing, rather than a commercial paradigm, and as a result impress statesmen abroad as being unexpectedly nonreciprocal. Some observers believe Japan practices "reverse engineering." In other words, a Japanese firm will buy a few exemplars of a new high-technology product from abroad, disassemble them to discover the technologies involved, and copy those technologies in manufacturing its own version of the product. It is then up to the foreign-patent holder to enforce his rights in Japan against the Japanese manufacturer, a process that is not necessarily easy or always successful.[28] There are also a few cases such as the famous Hitachi Spy Incident in which Japanese corporations have used what amount to undercover spy techniques to acquire proprietary technologies, usually by paying off an employee of a foreign corporation.[29]

The strategy of acquiring technology abroad on favorable terms appears sometimes to entail minimizing the claims of foreign-patent holders against Japanese corporations. Japan's patent office, as it happens, is actually one of MITI's subordinate departments, one of its "external bureaus." Patent officials are employees of the MITI planners.[30] Planners are thus in a position, if they choose, to bring strategic priorities to bear on patent policy. Some observers note that, in practice, Japanese patents are registered promptly and foreign patents are registered with glacial bureaucratic slowness and in this way delayed sometimes for as much as 10 years, enough time for a state-of-the-art product to have become an obsolete one.[31] There is some evidence that Japanese corporations practice parallel patenting. In other words, corporations have their engineers redesign a newly patented device slightly, just enough so they can claim their version lies outside the foreign-patent protection.[32]

Close kin to this is the strategy of patent flooding. The Japanese corporation examines the Western patent, and its engineers devise all manner of small changes, looking for design improvements. All of these minute modifications are patented, thus generating hundreds of patents for the Japanese corporation that are closely related to the original invention. Any modification that the original inventor tries to patent is likely to run afoul of the flood of Japanese patents. This process is likely to have the effect of giving the Japanese corporation more legal right to the technology than the original inventor has.[33]

Another source of technologies is co-production agreements with the United States to manufacture military equipment. Since the U.S. occupation ended in 1952, the U.S. government has sought to build up defense technologies and defense production in Japan. Japan builds all manner of high-technology armaments, ships, vehicles, artillery, missiles, and so on for its Self Defense Forces. Perhaps most advantageous to Japan for technology transfer, however, is military aircraft production.[34] Numerous advanced technologies have been made available to Japan by the U.S. government so that Japan could produce military planes. Japan manufactures almost all the military aircraft for its own use, at technology levels that are virtually state of the art.

The production agreements for these aircraft, amounting to a one-way transfer of advanced technologies from the United States, are a source of technologies that in practice seem sometimes to have flowed to Japanese civilian industries. F-104 fighter technology provided the braking system for Japan's bullet trains. The F-86F hydraulic systems provided technology for Japanese fire truck hoses. A U.S. aviation gyroscope stabilized Japanese-made seismographs and bowling alley equipment.[35] The most widely reported case, of course, has been that of the F-15 fighter aircraft and the MU-300. In 1982, shortly after assembly lines for the F-15 had been set up in Japan, Mitsubishi Heavy Industries began producing another aircraft on the same assembly lines, the MU-300. This was a corporate jet carrying 9 to 11 passengers. It was apparently a redesigned, commercialized version of the F-15, utilizing avionics, instrumentation, and propulsion technologies transferred through the F-15 program. It was marketed for a time in the United States by Mitsubishi Aircraft International, based in San Angelo, Texas. This was in a sense fitting since the United States had provided the technology.[36]

Licensing the F-15 to Japan required the passing of scores of advanced technologies worth billions from particular U.S. corporations to particular Japanese corporations. U.S. companies were directed by the U.S. government to hand over both the technologies and the licenses to produce them to their Japanese counterparts. The U.S. government saw to it, in law and in fact, that these expensive technologies were all transferred. McDonnell was instructed to license Daicel to produce F-15 aircraft assemblies. F-15 simulators were licensed by Goodyear Aerospace to Mitsubishi Precision. Technology for electrochemical machining of parts was transferred from TRW to Ishikawajima Harima Heavy Industries. Altitude indicators were handed from Rockwell to Tokyo Aircraft of Japan. Fuel transfer pumps went from TRW to Mitsubishi Heavy Industries. Instruments and transceivers passed from Bendix to Hokushin Electric. Wheel and brake components were conveyed from Bendix to Kayaba Industries. Direction finders were handed from Rockwell to Mitsubishi Electric. And so on.[37] Japan did, on the insistence of the U.S. government, sign an agreement in 1983 to transfer back to the United States military technologies Japan had developed, though it is still not clear what the practical consequences of this agreement will be.[38]

Technology is an essential element of any techno-industrial production system. Japanese planners use many means, at the interface and abroad, to acquire it. Some of these methods might impress many observers as more common in the domain of strategic activity than of commercial activity.

Japanese planners exercise other functions at the interface besides export promotion, market access, materials acquisition, and technologies acquisition, notably, favorable regulation of flows of funds. Nonetheless, a brief exploration of Japanese methods at the interface with respect to exports, markets, materials, and technologies is perhaps sufficient both to show that Japanese activities at the economic portal are guided by a consistent purpose and to gain some insight into what that purpose might be.

Operations Abroad

The objective of Japan's international strategy is apparently to gain strategic production and the factors of production. The main factors of production obtainable abroad include stable demand for consumers' and producers' goods; industrial materials and agricultural products; technology; capital flows; supplemental semiskilled labor; and demand for services, construction, and transport. We have seen what the policy of factor acquisition entails within Japan and at the portal. What does this strategy imply for Japanese operations abroad, however? This inquiry will not attempt to describe all of Japan's extensive operations around the globe but merely to convey some idea of the methods and principles that Japan tends to employ in certain national contexts abroad.

Structured Environments: Brazil

Abroad, as at home and at the interface, Japanese planners do not rely on markets alone. Rather, they tend to rely as well on institutional structures to create an environment favorable for implementation of their objectives. Abroad, as at the portal, they employ strategic means for strategic ends.

At home MITI relies on elaborate organizational structures, as we have seen, and also enjoys influence over the legal context, the opportunity to restructure whole industries, and the active cooperation of government and people, among other major advantages. When operating abroad, MITI does not enjoy these advantages. Nonetheless, if the foreign milieu in question seems to be a major source of factors of production and MITI expects to be active there for some time, it tends to establish institutional structures for the purpose of achieving policy objectives. These arrangements in some ways resemble those at home, though of course they are less elaborate. We cannot here explore all of Japan's extensive economic operations around the globe. By way of illustration, however, let us consider the structural arrangements in Brazil.

At the top of the Japan-in-Brazil system is the globally omnipresent MITI. MITI has three establishments located in Brazil. One of these is the MITI secretariat in the embassy in Brasília. The two others are JETRO offices, the JETRO São Paolo Center and the JETRO Rio de Janeiro Office. In addition to this, there are four groups of Brazil specialists in MITI departments in Tokyo, in the Oceania–Latin American Office of the International Trade Policy Bureau, in the Export Credit Insurance Division, in the Foreign Exchange Division, and in the Institute of Developing Economies.[39]

Also present in Brazil, not surprisingly, are 9 of Japan's 10 general trading companies, representing every major neo-zaibatsu.[40] The respective general trading companies, like MITI, have a regional headquarters in São Paolo or Rio and one in Tokyo.[41] Much of the trading companies' business in Brazil is in the purchase of bulk iron ore, soybeans, poultry, coffee, cotton, and other primary commodities. MITI controls the flow of these materials in Brazil by limiting each Brazilian seller to one Japanese buyer, and by assigning the buyer quotas. For example, all Brazilian iron ore bound for Japan must be sold to Nippon Steel. This promotes economies of scale and also gives the Japanese buying agency increased influence over prices offered by suppliers.[42]

Beneath the giant trading companies in Japan's economic hierarchy in Brazil are the Brazilian joint venture companies the trading companies own. Even when the Japanese corporations hold only minority positions in these ventures, they are sometimes able to orchestrate their production by controlling technology installation, operation, and maintenance. It is significant that Japanese owners of foreign manufacturing facilities sometimes retain de facto control over the producers' technology. Japanese officials may move the technology geographically but otherwise not lose effective control over it. The Japanese may carry out technological installation, maintenance, repair, replacement, and upgrades. In sum, Japanese technicians can and do sometimes operate producers' equipment that the host population may not be able to operate.[43]

Trading companies prefer to use indigenous representatives from their Brazilian companies to intercede for their interests in the local community. Fifteen of Brazil's major exporting firms, in steel, textiles, and aluminum, are owned by Japan.[44] In other words, there is a chain of techno-industrial orchestration that reaches from MITI to these and other Brazilian firms.

Besides structures for implementation and the institutional regulation of materials flows, the Japanese presence in Brazil also relies on expediting the flow of investment capital. Six percent of Japan's global direct foreign investment is in Brazil. The Japanese trading companies themselves are conduits of investment capital for development projects that serve their interests. Funds to support activities in Brazil also come from the EIBJ, the OECF, and other Japanese government financial agencies. One-third of Japan's loans to Brazil are through Japanese government institutions. Projects considered recently for loans include a superport at Tubarão and linkage of Brazil by rail to the Pacific.[45] Major input of Japanese government-controlled funds is one of the methods by which Japanese planners develop their objectives in Brazil.

Japanese officials use the same basic means in Brazil that they do at home: instructions to responsible institutions, orchestration of funds, and orchestration of materials. The difference is that they influence only some of these things in Brazil, not the preponderance of them, as at home. Moreover, local governments and populations are almost automatically sympathetic to MITI's strategic goals at home, which is not always the case in Brazil.

Having examined Japan's means in the Brazilian environment, let us consider its policy ends. What do Japanese officials seek to achieve there? Not surprisingly, Japanese interests in Brazil seek to secure factors of production for Japan, namely industrial raw materials, semiprocessed materials, certain agricultural products, and markets for producers' goods. Japan began by establishing long-term contracts with Brazil for purchasing raw materials and moved from that to ownership of the raw materials sources in Brazil. In some cases Japan mined and processed the materials itself where those activities had not been done before. In other words, much of Japan's investment capital went into developing new mines in Brazil. This was partially to serve Japan's growing requirement for strategic materials, such as iron ore, and in part to diversify its sources of those materials.[46]

Besides importing raw materials, Japan imports some semiprocessed materials from Brazil, such as ferroalloys. The reason for this apparently is that electricity, needed in large quantities to make these alloys, is cheaper in Brazil. In effect, Japan is importing bottled electrical energy by buying these alloys already processed. Electricity itself is a kind of raw material for which Japanese industry has a growing demand. Japan sometimes imports processed aluminum rather than bauxite as a way of utilizing other nations' less expensive energy. The object here is, in effect, to import energy as a raw material.[47]

In addition to industrial materials and energy, Japan draws agricultural materials from Brazil. Brazil is the world's largest exporter of soy meal. Virtually all of this soy production stems from heavy Japanese investment in Brazil's Cerrado region from 1974 to 1976, immediately after the U.S. soy embargo against Japan in 1973. In these years Brazil's annual soybean output grew from 20,000 bushels to 400 million bushels, a remarkable increase. This development has allowed Brazil to become a major global supplier of soybeans, much of the crop being shipped to Japan.[48] This approach, developing almost half a billion bushels of supply where there had been almost none, shows Japan's tendency to achieve its goals not only by reliance on passive factor endowments but also through strategic policy.[49]

Japan might be thought of as acquiring semiskilled labor abroad. Mobilizing foreign labor in plants abroad allows Japan to extend the effect of its own finite work force. This does not have an antiwelfarist effect at home because Japan strives always to upgrade its finite home production into ever-higher-value-added industries, leaving behind such labor-intensive activities as textile weaving. Labor itself, obviously an essential factor of production, is one of the things Japan's international strategy seems to seek abroad.

Japan has found markets in Brazil for its producers' durables. Japan sometimes exports complete manufacturing plants, turnkey factories, to Brazil and other developing nations. Ordinarily when Japan does this, the production created serves markets to which Japan had not had access. Japan thus gains the markets for the producers' durables without losing any markets for its products.[50] In the early 1960s, Japan began for the first time to establish textile production plants in Brazil, using Japanese equipment under Japanese management. This was subsequent to the Long-Term Arrangement Regarding International Trade in Cotton Textiles of October 1962, which limited textile exports from Japan directly to the United States.[51] Goods produced in this kind of relocated plant almost never displace Japanese goods. They are sold within a newly expanding local market that may have been closed by nationalist sentiment to Japanese goods or they are re-exported to third markets that for any reason may have been closed to Japan-produced goods. Foreign production by Japanese corporations serves usually to address markets that would not otherwise have been available to Japan.[52]

A major advantage of decisively influencing a foreign manufacturing operation is that the Japanese can direct its demand for producers' durables toward Japanese high-tech equipment makers. The opportunity to sell producers' durables may be a major motive for the Japanese acquiring certain industrial companies abroad. Most forms of production employ a spectrum of technologies. Japanese managers attempt to keep the high-end technologies, producers' technologies, in their hands, even when they are engaged in labor-intensive production in other nations. One of the factors of production Japan has sought with some success to secure in Brazil is markets for producers' durables.[53]

Japan seeks to acquire for itself in Brazil a broad range of production factors, as we have seen. These include industrial and agricultural materials, energy, labor, and markets for producers' goods. Japan also seeks in Brazil markets for certain high-end corporate services, such as brokerage in international sales and industrial financing. Japanese trading companies use their highly developed global distribution networks to exert influence over Brazilian firms and at the same time use Brazilian markets to accommodate trading interests of third nations. The giant trading companies do a great deal of third-country trade. They trade in "complementarities."[54] They bring to third nations what they need of each other's goods, thereby creating contacts and patterns of gratitude or obligation, at relatively little cost to the trading companies themselves or to Japan.[55]

Japan has sought to make Brazil into an environment favorable for implementation of its strategic objectives. Brazil is expected to provide industrial materials, energy, agricultural goods, labor, and demand for high-technology producers' goods and for services. To this end Japan supports a hierarchy of coordination in Brazil somewhat similar to the one it supports in Japan: MITI, neo-zaibatsu-linked general trading companies, and numerous Brazilian client corporations. Moreover, Japan uses some of the same levers of coordination that it uses at home—direct instruction, orchestration of funds, and orchestration of materials—although Japan cannot employ these methods abroad as extensively as at home. Although we are not in a position here to examine Japan's far-flung economic operations around the world, it is probably safe to assume that, besides in Brazil, Japan employs similar institutional arrangements in a considerable number of nations in which it has a substantial interest in acquiring production or factors of production.

Operations Abroad: Export Campaigns

Japan, when pursuing its strategic objectives on a long-term basis in foreign countries, tends to set up implementing structures rather than rely on existing markets. These arrangements in themselves may not be sufficient to meet all of Japan's strategic goals, however. With respect to the objective of obtaining increases in consumer production for Japan, all these structural approaches can do is create a favorable climate. Ultimately, Japanese companies, to move consumer production to Japan, must operate in foreign markets and serve individual foreign consumers. They must sell large numbers of their products abroad. This is achieved through export campaigns, one product at a time, with the same product often being sold in many places simultaneously around the world. The con-

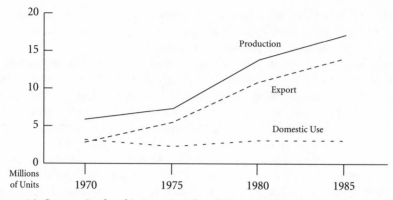

Figure 6.2 *Cameras Produced in Japan in Selected Years, Numbers Domestically Distributed and Numbers Exported*
SOURCE: *Japan Statistical Yearbook*. Statistics Bureau ed. Tokyo: Japan Statistical Association, 1988, pp. 243, 344.

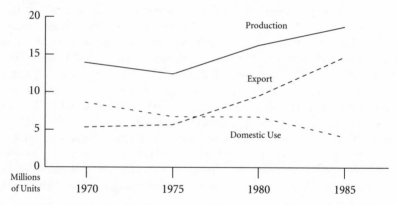

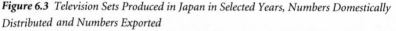

Figure 6.3 *Television Sets Produced in Japan in Selected Years, Numbers Domestically Distributed and Numbers Exported*
SOURCE: *Japan Statistical Yearbook*. Statistics Bureau ed. Tokyo: Japan Statistical Association, 1988, pp. 239, 344.

tours and scale of some of these campaigns can be seen in Figures 6.2, 6.3, and 6.4. The thing to note here is that in the course of global export campaigns for strategic products, domestic consumption may remain constant or fall slightly while total production and export distribution climb together to levels considerably above those of domestic consumption. The symmetry of this pattern across a broad range of products suggests that this is evidently the planners' policy. Market saturation probably constrains domestic consumption above a certain essential level, though planners may also contribute to this constraint either by influencing prices upward or by restricting the quantity of goods available for sale. The production pattern is apparently rationalized for international sales rather than exclusively for domestic consumer sales.

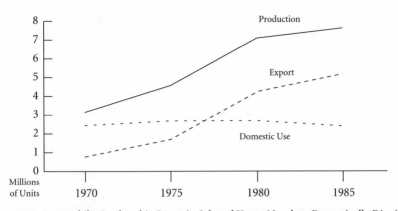

Figure 6.4 *Automobiles Produced in Japan in Selected Years, Numbers Domestically Distributed and Numbers Exported*
SOURCE: *Japan Statistical Yearbook.* Statistics Bureau ed. Tokyo: Japan Statistical Association, 1988, pp. 240, 345.

Export Campaigns: Some Principles

Japanese international economic activities are not necessarily adversarial in all their aspects. In the realm of export campaigns, however, these activities may be adversarial because they usually engage the same global markets that non-Japanese corporations do. Many Western commentators, either implicitly or explicitly, use military metaphors to describe dynamics of the export campaigns, and indeed it appears that some of this activity can be described rather more readily with the language of military engagement than with the more usual language of commerce. Admittedly, use of this military language amounts to an extended metaphor. Nonetheless, such a metaphor may be a useful way to achieve some conceptual insights into how the export campaigns work.

Japanese business leaders are well known for their interest in the classical Chinese military thinker Sun Tzu, the insightful Asian articulator of the principles of war. Many of the principles Sun Tzu enunciated are commonplaces of early-modern military thought in Western Europe as well, the classical Western formulator being Antoine de Jomini, Napoleonic veteran and theorist. Most modern military services publish "principles of war" that are largely later adaptations drawn from Jominian concepts. In the U.S. Army today the nine principles of war are mass, objective, security, surprise, maneuver, offensive, unity of command, simplicity, and economy of force.[56]

The principles of war are of interest because some aspects of Japan's export campaigns appear to resonate with some of these same principles. The concepts in play here are simple, and accessible by common sense or through popular games. B.H. Liddell Hart's brilliant summary of them is still the best: Concentrate your strength against the adversary's weakness.[57] Even so, Napoleonic warfare, the locus classicus in the West, provides a useful explanatory metaphor for these principles.

In a typical Napoleonic campaign, Napoleon determined the decisive military objective that would gain his political objective: the enemy's center of gravity, usually his army or capital. Napoleon then mobilized and secured his own re-source base and lines of communication and moved his armies toward the enemy. He seized the initiative and went on the offensive to keep enemies off balance and ensure a result favorable to himself. He used cavalry and direction of march to threaten to interdict, or actually to interdict, the enemies' lines of communica-tion, denying them their resource base. When he reached the vicinity of the en-emy, Napoleon concentrated his forces into an overwhelming mass and attacked smaller, fragmented enemy forces. Napoleon brought the bulk of his own forces to bear successively on parts of the enemies' forces to overcome them piecemeal or drive them from the field. This meant marching rapidly to intercept separate enemy armies before they could unite. If the foe had as much or more force on the field than Napoleon did, Napoleon would attack through the middle of the ene-my's line to break it into parts that he then could attack and defeat separately. Once he had engaged enemy forces, Napoleon controlled all arms himself to en-sure coordination of all assets for maximum effect. To break the enemy line, he would attack it where it was weakest: an exposed flank, a gap, wherever the line seemed thin. He delivered a firm blow at this weak point to create an opening in the enemy line. He poured forces through this opening into the enemy's rear ar-eas, causing enemy formations to dissolve and flee. Napoleonic cavalry could then pursue and easily defeat the dispersed elements of the adversary's force.[58]

There are many principles at work here, center of gravity, concentration and mass, security of lines, initiative, unity of command, bringing the bulk of one's as-sets to bear on lesser assets of the enemy, and others. Napoleonic warfare has passed into history, but the principles he used in campaigning have a larger appli-cability and are, in greatly abstracted form, still used by military theorists. Japa-nese export campaigns, like Napoleon's campaigns, appear to have a strategic pur-pose and to be strategically coordinated. They employ different resources than Napoleon did, obviously, but nevertheless, the concepts that seem to guide the ex-port activity resonate curiously with the concepts that guided Napoleon's cam-paigns.

The principles used by Japanese planners to get maximum strategic effect from finite assets bear a recognizeable conceptual similarity to some of the classical principles of military engagement. Let us explore some of these Japanese eco-nomic applications by following Japanese planners through a typical export drive. The same basic strategy has been used, so far, for textiles, steel, ships, autos, electronics, optics, and computers, and this strategy may be used in future for products still uninvented. The first step in this strategic process, in some ways the most important step, is to determine the strategic objective, the "decisive point," or "center of gravity" at the strategic level. Unless Japanese planners make the right call on this, their costly campaign, even if successful, will not further strategic ends. They must choose a goal that is attainable, given their existing capabilities and real-world conditions. They must choose the industrial sector that will most enhance their productive capacity, wealth, and political influence; that will best position them for further development; and that Japan actually has the resources to enter.[59] Because of these criteria, it is easy to predict their decisions. Japanese strategists consistently choose industries for development that lie at the next higher level of technology from where Japan's capabilities currently lie, and for which there exists an established and accessible world market. Their objective then is to rapidly develop industries in this sector for sale in world markets. In the 1970s, Japanese planners chose as their objective "knowledge-intensive" industries, that is, the semiconductor industry and industries such as computers and robots that used semiconductors. The purpose of this campaign, in MITI's words, was to develop Japanese industries' "international superiority" and "form a foundation for the long-term development of the economy and society."[60] Knowledge-intensive industries are only a recent instance. Japanese planners earlier had focused on textiles, steel, optics, and much else, and most likely there will be similar focuses in decades to come. Like any good strategic planner, MITI officials strive to identify the "decisive point," the attainable operational goal that will realize strategic ends.

Having selected the decisive point, planners honor the principle of concentration. They honor this principle first in the sense of bringing to bear all of Japan's available investment capital on the production sector involved. As Yoshihisa Ojimi, a recent head of MITI, put it, "According to Napoleon and Clausewitz, the secret of a successful strategy is concentration of fighting power on the main battle grounds; fortunately ... Japan has been able to concentrate its scant capital in strategic industries."[61] By focusing the nation's capital resources on a selected industry, MITI can rapidly develop world-class production technology and double capacity every few years to achieve economies of scale. Not all of the nation's savings are allowed to drift randomly. Some savings are guided by public officials and dedicated to the favored strategic-industrial sectors on whose development the nation's future may seem to depend.

Japan is famous for developing production in protected domestic markets. Several of the classical operational principles are at work here, including rear-area security and "concentration and mass." In the secure home environment, before engaging world markets, planners gather productive assets in the chosen sector. They develop low-cost, high-volume, high-value production at home before attempting to export, often in an environment largely free of exposure to imports. Planners take care to achieve economies of scale and superior production capabilities before they engage non-Japanese corporations abroad. This is possible in part because Japanese operators are often able to exclude major foreign interests from the home market area, where this crucial initial buildup takes place.[62] This sheltered home market keeps foreign interests from using Japanese resources and allows Japanese strategists to fully mobilize all of the resources of the home market. Moreover, exclusion of non-Japanese institutions keeps them from diluting the domestic pattern of coordination. Japan represents a secure resource base for strategic operations abroad. It is tantamount to the "zone-of-the-interior," the homeland, in military operations. A military commander can sally forth from a secure base, engage, and return to the protected base in an emergency or to refit for his next campaign. Japanese leaders, in effect, use their exclusive home markets in this way. They use the large home market not only to prepare and resource each new techno-industrial campaign, but also repair to this base in case a campaign fails. When an export drive falters, planners stop exporting and shift to new product or production designs in the shelter of home before mounting another drive. The domestic market, being perimetered, allows Japanese operators to be "insulated from foreign competition" and "cushioned ... from ... market errors."[63] Japanese operators maintain "zone-of-the- interior" security, an advantage in a strategic contest.

Once techno-industrial assets in a sector are sufficiently developed at home, that is, when mass is achieved, Japanese officials seize the initiative. They mount an export drive in the strategic sector. They thus in effect go on the offensive and catch adversaries off balance. They do not tarry and hope that random events or actions by the adversary will somehow advance their goals. Rather they cleave to the principle of the offensive. They seize the initiative themselves to guarantee that their goals are met.

When commencing an export drive, Japanese officials appear to prefer to engage non-Japanese corporate adversaries initially where those adversaries are not strongly represented. Japanese officials develop production first for sheltered domestic markets where non-Japanese interests are unrepresented or underrepresented. They then move into markets in third world countries where low-end goods in a given sector, say electronics, are acceptable to consumers. These low-end markets are often regarded as being of only marginal importance by non-Japanese industrial corporations, so these corporations tend not to contest such markets. After further developing economies of scale and revenue flows in the third world environments, the Japanese export campaign moves on to low-end niches in the home markets of industrial corporate adversaries. The Japanese target certain carefully selected parts of the adversary corporations' markets that are not being well serviced by those corporations, or they target parts of the market where Japan's still-developing industries are already competitive. They choose niches where they have a localized superiority of capability. Moreover, they choose low-end niches that are again apt to be viewed by adversary corporations as marginal and that are therefore left uncontested. Like Napoleon, they engage the adversary's

defenses where they are thin. This low-end presence once more enhances economies of scale and revenue flows for further development of capacity. At this point,
Japanese strategists control all the Japanese market in the targeted sector, part of
the third world market, and part of the non-Japanese adversary corporation's
home market. At this point, and only at this point, when the adversary's home
markets are already entered and when a superior mass of assets is already developed, Japanese strategists launch full-scale export campaigns against the corporate adversary's home markets in the selected sector. That is, they inundate the
corporate adversary's market with high-quality, low-priced goods.[64]

Napoleon preferred to engage his adversaries piecemeal. Japanese planners take
advantage of the fact that non-Japanese corporations are often not strategically
coordinated above the corporate level. Japanese planners are thus able to bring
the bulk of their resources to bear on the uncoordinated and thus isolated assets
of their competitors. Non-Japanese corporations that are not coordinated or
resourced on a national scale must rely on strategies that are far less abundantly
leveraged on a percentage of revenues from their own sales. Strategies that enjoy
access to nationally coordinated financial resources can often overcome strategies
leveraged on one corporation's net profit. These targeted corporations are routinely frustrated by the concentration and mass applied by Japanese planners,
who bring the bulk of their national resources to bear on corporate rivals who
may not enjoy the advantage of being coordinated above the corporate level. In
other words, Japanese planners prevail in part because they engage their adversaries piecemeal.

Japanese export campaigns appear to follow certain principles, which resonate
interestingly with the classical principles of military operations that one finds in
Sun Tzu or in the Napoleonic theorist Jomini. The classical operational principles
that seem to be represented in the Japanese export campaigns include selection of
the strategic center of gravity as objective, concentration and mass, security of the
resource base, initiative, and use of the bulk of one's assets against lesser assets of
the adversary. Like so many features of Japan's strategic-economic system, the dynamics of Japan's export campaigns are difficult to explain with a strictly commercial lexicon. Some of these dynamics seem easier to explain with reference to
the classical operational principles that are more commonly found in the conceptual vocabulary of national security.

Domestic Strategy and Global Strategy

Japan's domestic strategic system and its global strategic system, though directed
by the single agency MITI, are nonetheless fundamentally distinct. They operate
under different conditions, have different purposes, and to some extent have different political constituencies among the Japanese public. The domestic and

global systems are not so much integrated and unified as they are compatible and coordinated.

The objective of the domestic system is social well-being and social peace. This is accomplished by providing an ever-improving abundance of attractive techno-industrial employments for persons of all classes, providing they are willing to dedicate themselves to the effort. Since the rewards, tangible and intangible, are generous and certain, it turns out that almost everyone is willing to dedicate himself or herself to the effort. The global strategic system evidently has as its ultimate political goal the enhancement of Japan's influence regionally and globally. The global economic goal that supports the political objective is the channeling of production and factors of production to Japan.

The essence of modern strategic organization is unity of ends and plurality of means: the coordination of many agencies for one purpose. Noteworthy in such a system are both the existence of the structures of coordination and the particular purpose, or objectives, for which they are being employed. The structure of coordination for the international dimension of Japan's strategic economy was explored in Chapter 5. The likely practical objectives of these agencies' activities are set forth in this chapter, namely a measure of international influence achieved by acquiring major factors of production.

By observing the activity of Japanese international economic agencies in securing production and factors of production at the interface—export promotion, market access, raw materials, and technology—it is fairly easy to deduce both the approximate nature of the objective and the fairly consistent pattern of coordination. In its operations abroad, Japan sometimes seems to establish a structural environment to help achieve its goals rather than to rely only on pre-existing markets. Japan also launches export campaigns abroad for selected products that appear to follow certain systematic principles. Growing scholarly interest and inquiry into the Japanese international economic system in recent decades has steadily yielded new evidence to confirm the tendency of certain elements of this system to exhibit strategic dynamics rather than exclusively commercial dynamics.

Notes

1. Edward N. Luttwak, *Strategy: The Logic of War and Peace* (Cambridge, MA: Belknap Press, 1987), p. 70.

2. A number of observers have addressed Japan's preoccupation with "economic security." See, for example, Leon Hollerman, *Japan's Economic Strategy in Brazil* (Lexington, MA: Lexington-Heath, 1988), p. 98; Clyde V. Prestowitz, *Trading Places* (New York: Basic Books, 1988), pp. 147–48; Organization for Economic Cooperation and Development, *The Industrial Policy of Japan* (Paris: OECD, 1972), p. 164.

3. Yoshio Suzuki, a Japanese financial official, observed in a recent study that "postwar economic policy was constructed with investment/export-led growth as its strategic objec-

tive. The important elements in the policy were trade ... management, protection of industry (etc.)." See Yoshio Suzuki, *Money, Finance, and Macroeconomic Performance in Japan* (New Haven: Yale University Press, 1986), p. 4. See also Ira C. Magaziner and Thomas M. Hout, *Japanese Industrial Policy* (Berkeley, CA: Institute of International Studies, 1980), pp. 93–96, for Japan's policy of protection at home and export abroad.

4. Richard E. Caves and Masu Uekusa, "Industrial Organization," pp. 459–523 in Hugh Patrick and Henry Rosovsky, eds., *Asia's New Giant* (Washington, DC: Brookings Institution, 1976), p. 488; Magaziner and Hout, p. 48.

5. Chalmers Johnson, *MITI and the Japanese Miracle* (Stanford, CA: Stanford University Press, 1982), p. 234.

6. Ibid., p. 235.

7. Ibid., pp. 234–35; Joseph A. Pechman, "Taxation," pp. 317–82 in Patrick and Rosovsky, p. 357.

8. Pechman, pp. 355–56.

9. Johnson, *MITI*, pp. 234–35; Pechman, p. 357.

10. Johnson, *MITI*, p. 234; T. J. Pempel, "Japanese Foreign Economic Policy: The Domestic Bases for International Behavior," pp. 723–74 in Peter J. Katzenstein, ed., *Between Power and Plenty: Foreign Economic Policies of Advanced Industrial Countries*, published as a special edition of *International Organization* 31.4 (Aut 77): 581–920 (whole volume); p. 749.

11. Pempel, p. 749; Pechman, p. 359. For some other tax benefits for exports, see also Magaziner and Hout, p. 97.

12. Alexander K. Young, *The Sogo Shosha: Japan's Multinational Trading Companies* (Boulder, CO: Westview Press, 1979), p. 129.

13. *Tsusan handobukku* [*MITI Handbook*], Tsusan handobukku henshu iinkai ed. [MITI Handbook Editing Committee ed.] (Tokyo: Shokokaikan, 1989) [hereafter *MITI Handbook*], pp. 59–62, 526.

14. For explanation of these categories, and for full texts of the enabling laws, see *Tsusho sangyo roppo* [*International Trade and Industry Laws*], Tsusho sangyo-sho ed. [MITI ed.] (Tokyo: Marui Kobunsha, 1988), pp. 165–77. For related regulations, see pp. 177–86.

15. Cf. Edward J. Lincoln, *Japan's Unequal Trade* (Washington, DC: Brookings Institution, 1990), p. 61.

16. Occasionally Japanese officials may admit the existence of a protection policy. See, for example, Suzuki, *Money, Finance*, p. 4.

17. Pempel, p. 747; Lincoln, p. 154.

18. Pempel, p. 764; Marvin J. Wolf, *The Japanese Conspiracy* (New York: Empire Books, 1983), p. 18.

19. Prestowitz, p. 95.

20. Ibid., pp. 131–33.

21. Lincoln, p. 146.

22. Magaziner and Hout, p. 62.

23. Hollerman, p. 228.

24. Kunio Yoshihara, *Sogo Shosha: The Vanguard of the Japanese Economy* (New York: Oxford University Press, 1982), p. 208; Charles J. McMillan, *The Japanese Industrial System* (Berlin: Walter de Gruyter, 1984), p. 103.

25. See Pempel, p. 746; McMillan, p. 219; Prestowitz, pp. 131–32; Wolf, p. 88.

26. Michael Borrus, James Millstein, and John Zysman, *U.S.–Japanese Competition in the Semiconductor Industry* (Berkeley, CA: Institute of International Relations, 1982), p. 114.

27. Ibid., pp. 49, 112. On robots, see McMillan, p. 219.

28. Wolf suggests that 5 percent of Japan's engineering resources may be devoted to "reverse engineering." Wolf, p. 48.

29. Ibid., p. 59.

30. For organization of the Japan Patent Office, see *MITI Handbook,* pp. 153–202.

31. Prestowitz, pp. 132, 177–78.

32. Consider, for example, Mitsubishi Electric's copying of the electrodeless microwave lamps of Fusion Systems Corporation of Rocksville, MD, making only slight changes. See Stephen K. Yoder, "Japan Patent Issue," *Wall Street Journal,* October 13, 1988, p. B4.

33. Cf. ibid. Mitsubishi Electric promptly filed 200 patents on electrodeless microwave lamps.

34. Cf. Pempel, p. 762.

35. Ibid.

36. Reinhard Drifte, *Arms Production in Japan* (Boulder, CO: Westview Press, 1986), p. 61.

37. Ibid., pp. 114–20.

38. Ibid., pp. 79–82. For the text of the technology transfer agreement, see pp. 95–100.

39. Hollerman, p. 100; *MITI Handbook,* pp. 39, 500, 506.

40. Hollerman, p. 15. The 9 trading companies in Brazil are among the 10 general trading companies that are described in Chapter 5, with Ataka and Co. being the only major trading concern with no presence in Brazil.

41. Ibid., p. 271.

42. Ibid., p. 228.

43. See ibid., p. 118.

44. Ibid., pp. 118, 120.

45. Ibid., pp. 15, 16, 22, 270.

46. Ibid., p. 99.

47. Ibid., p. 123.

48. Ibid., pp. 225–26.

49. Compare ibid., p. 267. Hollerman points out that Japan has changed the shape of the Brazilian economy in several ways.

50. Magaziner and Hout, p. 52; McMillan, p. 233.

51. Hollerman, p. 117.

52. Compare ibid., p. 118.

53. Ibid., pp. 99, 117, 269.

54. Ibid., p. 18.

55. Ibid., pp. 18, 270.

56. See Sun Tzu, *The Art of War,* Samuel B. Griffith tr. (London: Oxford University Press, 1963); Sun Tzu, R. L. Wing tr., *The Art of Strategy* (New York: Doubleday, 1988); Antoine-Henri de Jomini, *Summary of the Art of War,* pp. 432–557 in Stackpole Books ed., *Roots of Strategy, Book* 2 (Harrisburg, PA: Stackpole Books, 1987), esp. p. 461; Antoine-Henri de Jomini, *The Art of War* (Novato, CA: Presidio Press, 1992); *Field Manual 100-5: Operations,* Headquarters Department of the Army ed. (Washington, DC: USGPO, 1986), pp. 173–82.

57. B.H. Liddell Hart, *Strategy* (New York: Meridian, 1991 [1954]), p. 334.

58. See David G. Chandler, *The Campaigns of Napoleon* (New York: Macmillan, 1966), pp. 161–91.

59. Borrus, Millstein, and Zysman, pp. 47, 111.

60. Ibid., pp. 4–5, 47, 111.

61. Quoted in Philip H. Trezise and Yukio Suzuki, "Politics, Government, and Economic Growth in Japan," pp. 753–811 in Patrick and Rosovsky, p. 793.

62. Borrus, Millstein, and Zysman, p. 52.

63. Ibid., pp. 6, 47, 52.

64. Ibid., p. 52.

PART THREE

CONCLUSION

7
Strategic Economy: Schumpeter, Napoleon, and Others

LET US ENDEAVOR here to sketch out the strategic portion of the Japanese economy in its essential outline. We will then be in a position to examine this system's dynamics in light of several philosophical and historical perspectives that have been developed by Western scholars. As we have seen, most of the Japanese economy, the quotidian economy, is private and commercial in nature. The remainder, however, namely a quarter or so of the economy, comprising mainly certain techno-industrial and financial activities, appears to have been brought under a pattern of public sponsorship. We will refer to this publicly sponsored quarter of the economy as Japan's strategic economy.

How should we characterize Japan's strategic economy? Economic policy in this sector is made rather in the same way diplomatic or military policy is made in the West, by highly motivated officials, with parliamentary and journalistic overview. Policy is devised by MITI, reviewed and accepted or not by the elected legislature, and then implemented through a complex structure of coordination supervised by MITI. Multilevel staffing and planning, running from the government above to the corporations below, are a vital element of the strategic-economic system's success. This distinctive arrangement of multilevel planning, and its being brought into the realm of national policy goals, are features that may make it appropriate to refer to this system as a strategic system.

Domestically, MITI orchestrates the economy in three ways: direct policy instruction, orchestration of major funds flows, and orchestration of certain materials flows. For each of these functions, MITI exercises its authority through a different set of mediating institutions. For direct instruction, MITI relies on neozaibatsu and on various industrial associations and cartels. For regulation of funds, MITI, through the MOF, depends primarily upon the Bank of Japan and the rest of the banking system, but also on the postal savings, insurance, taxation, and pricing systems. For coordination of materials, MITI works principally through public policy companies, the quasi-private legal monopolies that handle certain categories of goods.

Beneath the great mediating institutions and guided by them are some 200 strategic corporations. These institutions differ in certain ways from other commercial corporations. Their stocks are cross-owned so that they are managerially answerable mainly to each other, in a pattern that amounts to managerial peer review. They might be viewed as being in effect collectively self-owned. There are about 30 corporations in each of six great interownership clusters, namely the six neo-zaibatsu groups: Mitsubishi, Mitsui, Sumitomo and so on. Each of the strategic corporations in turn has numerous affiliated client companies; there are some 10,000 of these affiliated firms all told.

This elaborate system thrives in part because of the ingenious limits and compromises that are built into it. Economic policy, while being made, is scrutinized by politicians and journalists. Although policy goals are set by MITI, strategic corporations at lower levels are free to employ any means they wish to achieve them, since discipline is accomplished through competition rather than micromanagement. Moreover, half or more of the economy, the nonstrategic quotidian economy, is left outside strategic policy entirely. We might not be too far off the mark in assuming that strategic institutions own one-fourth of the economy and influence part of an additional one-fourth, thus leaving the remaining half or more of the economy as purely quotidian, private and commercial, and outside the orbit of strategic orchestration altogether.

Care is taken not to disturb the normal vigorous functioning of markets by using only "market conforming" methods. Public policy companies do not abridge markets and instead emulate normal market participants. Strategic corporations are legally autonomous in their internal operations, preventing government micromanagement. The orchestrated system, being wedded to these sophisticated limits, seems to realize simultaneously both the advantages of a planned system and those of a competitive market system. Japan's strategic economy handily outperforms both free-market and planned systems by freely deploying elements of both.

In the domestic sphere, Japan's strategic system has achieved remarkable results. The policy objective has seemed to be to continuously both increase production and upgrade the technological level of production. In fact, Japan's GDP doubled every few years between 1952 and 1973. For individuals, this has meant satisfying and constantly improving employment opportunities, and incomes. Unemployment has remained below 3 percent, and poverty (except for a tiny percentage of true misfits) has largely disappeared. The domestic strategy seems to have a welfarist constituency and welfarist aims and results. It provides social well-being, social peace, and, indeed, brisk social mobility for everyone. In this benign milieu, many dreams come true.

Japan's international economic strategy is another matter. The international strategy has different purposes, constituencies, and instrumentalities than does the domestic one. The international strategy and the domestic strategy are technically compatible but still distinct. The purpose of the international strategy is not to provide better employments and incomes for millions of citizens, though it is compatible with those ends.

The ultimate political purpose of the international economic strategy is apparently to increase Japan's diplomatic influence. Without such a presumption it is difficult to explain one major feature of the Japanese system: It produces but does not consume. Japan's international strategy furthers the political object of increasing Japanese influence by moving production and factors of production to Japan. This activity, naturally, serves the interest of the political public that underwrites it and under some circumstances may be adversarial. It is nearly global in scope. It is engaged in at times by all strategic agencies of the Japanese government, not just by the economic ones. It has a measure of publicly controlled funding behind it. This activity's apparent objective is to preserve and augment national influence. It appears to be carried on for purposes analogous to those for which modern diplomatic and military systems are maintained and, like those systems, has a coordinating structure and employs public funds.

The international economic coordination structure is analogous to the domestic economic coordination structure. MITI at the top devises policy and orchestrates implementation. It works at the next level through general trading companies and their affiliated client corporations. MITI guides the flow of funds through the Export Import Bank of Japan and guides the flow of materials through public policy companies and in some cases cartels or industrial associations. Economic policy is coordinated with other policy levers: diplomatic, intelligence, and others. In practice, diplomatic, intelligence, and other activities appear at times to be subordinated to strategic-economic goals, perhaps because Japanese leaders believe it is only in the economic area that important advantages can be achieved for Japan under existing circumstances.

Japan's global economic strategy appears to operate at multiple levels, perhaps six distinct ones, for both planning and implementation. Coordination in this international system, as in the domestic one, is in principle noninterventionist. The global strategy operates in three zones: domestic, interface (at the portal between Japan and the world), and abroad. The domestic zone increases production and restrains consumption, thus creating a surplus for export. The interface zone is a critical locus for the regulation of flows of funds and goods in global strategic operations. In economic activities abroad Japan sometimes establishes a structured environment favorable to its goals, similar in some ways to that at home. Japan also launches vigorous global drives to export carefully selected products. Japanese planners seem to systematically employ certain operational principles in these global campaigns. Japan's global economic strategy to date has been a major technical success, given the purposes it is apparently meant to serve.

The Japanese system encompasses two strategies, one domestic, the other international. These strategies, and the institutions that operate them, are interactive but distinct. The object of the domestic strategy is to provide ever-more-rewarding employments, livelihoods, and lives to all members of Japanese society. Japanese people's dreams come true. The apparent object of the international strategy is to achieve a degree of diplomatic influence in the international community. Japan's domestic and international strategies employ some of the same institutional methods and are fashioned, in fact, by the same government agency, MITI. Even so, they have different purposes and consequences. This brief survey should put us in a position now to approach some of the major features of the Japanese system in a more reflective way.

Joseph Schumpeter: Policy-Market Economy

Japanese leaders appear to have developed a new relationship between government and certain industries, a government-industry partnership that amounts to taking these industries under a kind of public sponsorship. The practices involved in this pattern are unfamiliar to us if taken in the ensemble. The major elements that make up the pattern, however, have almost all been established for some time in Western scholarship, in Western practice, or both. The Japanese system may not be as unfamiliar and inaccessible to us as it might at first appear. In the world of contemporary practice, as we have seen, most of the Japanese methods can be found either in the realm of Western commerce or in the realm of other institutional environments. In the realm of scholarship, most of the major elements of the Japanese system can also be found in the Western literature. Although there is no single scholar or thinker in the West that exactly describes the Japanese economic system, the major features of that remarkable system can almost all be found described somewhere or other by Western scholars and thinkers. Examining the major attributes of the Japanese system as they appear in Western scholarship may help us improve our awareness of those attributes. Four intellectual figures will be useful to us for this exercise: Joseph Schumpeter (1883–1950), Friedrich List (1789–1846), Napoleon Bonaparte (1769–1821) (that is, his historical interpretors), and Adam Smith (1723–1790). Simply put, Schumpeter offers insights into the reconciliation of policy and markets; List indicates the advantages of production; Napoleonic practice illumines the qualities of strategic organization; and Smith explains the importance of limits.

Let us begin with Schumpeter. Domestically, Japan's strategic economy blends laissez-faire and interventionist elements. Most conventional economists in the West do not routinely reflect on the possible benefits of combining interventionist and noninterventionist practices. There is at least one economist of established reputation in the West who does describe such an arrangement, however, namely the Austrian-born Harvard economist Joseph Schumpeter. Schumpeter, in *Capitalism, Socialism and Democracy* (1942), outlined as an academic exercise an economic system in which "the economic affairs of society belong to the public, not to the private sphere." Control over production would be "vested with a central authority," namely a "Central Board or Ministry of Production," which in turn would report to an elected "congress or parliament." These features notwithstanding, this system would operate in such a way that considerable "freedom of action" would be left to "the managers of the individual industries or plants."[1]

In Schumpeter's system, the Ministry of Production would plan for continuous improvement of productive capacity. "Progress itself" would be "mechanized." "Innovation" would be "reduced to routine." "Planning for progress" would be the rule and would provide for "the systematic coordination and orderly distribution in time of new ventures in all lines." Planning by the Ministry of Production would make it possible for "each industrial board," namely the management of each industry, to make its plans accordingly.[2]

In spite of all this planning, however, most of the economic activity in the society would still rely on markets. The main features of traditional market systems would remain vigorous, including capital accumulation, savings, interest, and wages. "The fundamental logic of economic behavior is the same" in both private commercial and mixed-policy economies, Schumpeter believed. Consumers' dollars would still establish demand. The system would be pluralistic, with many decisions made by various groups of managers in the respective industries, who would be controlled largely by the Ministry of Production's "allocating productive resources" rather than by rigid instruction only.[3]

Schumpeter's theoretical system might be described as a policy-market economy, meaning that public policy provided the ends and that markets provided the means. It is important to remember, however, that Schumpeter's system was entirely academic. Schumpeter was trying to imagine what forms industrial organization might take at some time in the future. Even so, Schumpeter's imagined system did anticipate several features of today's Japanese system, namely, that it might be possible to impose a degree of policy coordination on markets without abridging or disrupting them, that such policy like any policy could be formulated by elected democratic bodies, and that success in such an arrangement might require supervision by a specialized agency, a "ministry of production."[4] In other words, Anglo-American readers who are interested in these attributes have some access to them in serious scholarship in their own tradition, scholarship that has been available for fifty years, and need not rely exclusively on new scholarship about Japan for an introduction to them.

Several important features of Japanese practice differ, however, from what is found in Schumpeter's academic system. The Japanese system, in both domestic and international spheres, seems to give priority to production, whereas Schumpeter seems to have thought that consumption would have priority. In

Schumpeter's system, there were only two or so levels of implementation, whereas Japan's system is characterized by multiple levels of implementation. Schumpeter assumed that the whole economy might eventually be taken up in the policy-market pattern, whereas in Japan, most of the economy seems to have been deliberately and perennially left out of this pattern. To help us with these omissions—production as priority, strategic organization, and limits—we will find it useful to examine some of the ideas of List, Napoleon, and Smith respectively.

Friedrich List: The Priority of Production

Japanese economic policies are believed by many observers to favor production over consumption and developing production over consuming products. This is true in Japan's international economic activity but also in its domestic economic activity. Giving priority to production implies a perspective on the Japanese part that production somehow has value that is independent of consumption or is more fundamental than consumption. The Western thinker who may come closest to providing such a perspective is Friedrich List. List was a western German political economist who was concerned mainly that the industrial development of his native Germany was being prevented by the influx of high-quality manufactured goods from Britain. He migrated to Philadelphia for a time and expressed similar concerns for nascent U.S. industry. Many Americans are familiar with concepts like List's through Alexander Hamilton's (1755–1804) *Report on Manufactures,* submitted to Congress in 1791. Still, we might do well to examine List's insights, since he addressed international production issues systematically as such. List advocated tariffs and a tariff union to allow the German states to develop modern industries despite the influx of superior British goods. List's prescriptions were eventually enacted a generation after his death and had reversed the industrial positions of the German and British empires by the end of the century.

List wrote his pilot study, *The Natural System of Political Economy,* in 1837, and his more comprehensive treatise, *The National System of Political Economy,* in 1841. What made List's thought unique was not his advocacy of tariffs, which was fairly common in his milieu, but the exceptional insights he had into why developmental tariffs were desirable. List saw the nation itself as a production system or an environment of production. The nation, and the individuals in it, prospered only if the nation's "productive powers" increased. It behooved the nation to use all the means at its disposal—tariffs, quotas, subsidies, diplomacy and so on—to make certain this happened. Under existing modern conditions, success in this effort was a prerequisite for national survival, he believed. Statesmen therefore needed to master political economy, which was precisely this study of how to shield, nourish, and increase the whole polity's productive powers, which was their responsibility. Political economy had to do with policy, structured incentives, and human capital. Accumulation of specie or commodities had no intrinsic value for List. Industrial production itself was the only value he recognized. Wise and persistent national policy was the only way a people could obtain it.[5]

List did not actually advocate that a nation should take over another nation's manufacturing. But he believed Britain historically had done something like this and directly owed its predominant geostrategic influence in the nineteenth century to its having done so. List advocated defensive pro-manufacturing policies without reservation, however. Though appropriating other nations' domestic production might be unseemly, a nation's producing what it itself consumed was not. A nation should use tariffs, quotas, and subsidies to encourage replacing imports with domestic manufactures. List had some unusual perspectives on why this was advantageous and necessary. It was fitting for a nation to do this, since individuals depended on the nation for "mental culture, power of production, security, and prosperity."[6] List evidently thought the same was true of particular industries, namely that they depended on the nation for a nourishing environment. Individual merchants could not always be counted on to fashion such an environment because they might make a profit regardless of the systemic effect of what they handled.[7]

Creating a favorable environment for industry must be done by some agency with a longer perspective in time than the individual producer is likely to have. This is because the effect of social investment in the short term is likely to be material austerity and deprivation. The fruit of sacrificial investment may come only decades or generations later. List said this is like a progressive farmer's investing in the education of his son, knowing full well the rewards will come only in the far future. He pointed to Holland's marvelous system of canals and dikes, which required many generations to build and perfect.[8] It was important to remember, according to List, that the object of developmental policies should be productive power itself, not the accumulation of specie or other commodity, which had no special value per se.[9]

The rewards for fostering productive powers, however, were great, and they were not just material rewards. For List, urban industrial society "called forth ... the growth of intellectual and moral forces of every kind." Industry was "the mother and father of science, literature, the arts, enlightenment, freedom, useful institutions, and national power and independence." Manufacturing towns allowed dreams to come true for entrepreneurs and skilled workers alike.[10] The dreams of nations might also be served or disserved by the degree to which policies favored productive powers. Successful practitioners could achieve political greatness. A nation's military power depended to an important extent on the degree to which it was industrialized. Moreover, a nation that relied on another to turn its raw materials into manufactured goods was vulnerable in case of strategic conflict.[11]

In other words, List longed for productive powers for the nation not because they represented "wealth" in the sense of material comfort but because they were uplifting culturally and socially and animated every sector of the society. The power, freedom, and cultural dignity of the nation as a whole also hinged on this. Productive powers made the dreams of individuals and nations come true. List's originality was not that he advocated tariffs for development. Instead, it lay in his commitment to use material means for grander cultural and political ends. Development of industrial production would lead to social happiness and greatness.

More than other Western notions, Listian developmentalism seems to explain several distinctive features of the Japanese system: the primacy of production, the crucial role of policy in fashioning a favorable environment for it, and some of the objectives of global economic policy.

Napoleon Bonaparte: Strategic Organization

List is useful for explaining certain features of the Japanese economy, but neither Schumpeter nor List accounts for the pattern of multilevel planning and coordination that characterizes the Japanese system. Japanese economic leaders' methods in supervising certain parts of the Japanese economy are new to us. It may nonetheless be possible for us to understand these methods without too much difficulty because they are analogous in some respects to methods used in modern strategic military organization. Conceptually, we may find that the resourceful Japanese methods are more accessible than we might at first have thought.

In this connection it may be helpful to briefly explore the origins of modern strategic military organization in the Western context. The essence of modern strategic organization is unity of ends and plurality of means, the former linked to the latter by a series of dedicated staff echelons. We tend to take strategic military organization for granted, as if it were an obvious universal solution that had always been with us. In fact, however, modern strategic organization in the West has origins that are historically both fairly identifiable and fairly specific.

In the early years of the French Revolution, French legislators made resources available for military activity on an unprecedented scale. Although French political leaders at the time may not have realized it, the stage was thereby set for the emergence of modern strategic organization. To put this more concretely, military emergencies caused a million men to flow into the French army in 1793, and the legislature did not hesitate to provide the funds to maintain them. The new republic, strategically challenged, had evidently solved its problem of finding increased resources, but the enormity of the solution generated other strategic and operational problems that were in themselves extremely daunting. In the event, the mobilization of citizen soldiers created overwhelming difficulties. How were these vast numbers of troops to be fed and supplied? How could they be deployed at once on many fronts against many foes? These dilemmas had to be resolved quickly if the new regime wished to survive. In fact, both the logistical and the operational problems were solved by the rapid and ingenious development of new organizational forms.

In the old dynastic armies, the regiment, about 2,000 men, was the largest permanent formation. In battle the commander just lined up his regiments facing the enemy. French officers in the 1790s, however, with unprecedented thousands to deploy, began inventing ever larger formations between the regiment and the state: the brigade (two regiments), the division (two or three brigades), the corps (two to four divisions). In addition there was the field army (two or more corps), frequently used, though not yet a permanent formation. All of these new organizations were created between the New Constitution of the Army in 1790 and the emergence of Napoleon as emperor in 1804. The practical effect was that armies that dwarfed the Sun King's could be sent off in all directions with a reasonable expectation of efficient supply and deployment.

At the simplest level, an increase in scale was the concept in play here. In reality there were several more-complex principles at work. The military inventors employed the principle of the quasi-autonomous self-sufficient microcosm. Each unit was deliberately heterogeneous in its assets. Each division was given its own infantry, artillery, logistical staff, commander, and headquarters. In other words, it was administratively, and for some purposes tactically, a self-sufficient microcosm of the army and could therefore act independently of other organizations. Similarly, the corps had infantry, cavalry, artillery, other specialized assets, and its own commander and headquarters. Each corps was a self-sufficient microcosm of the whole army. A corps could do anything the army could do, both administratively and tactically. It was tailored, in fact, to engage an enemy field army. Creating armies in complete microcosm had important advantages. It meant a corps could operate autonomously at any time. It drastically simplified what had appeared to be insurmountable problems of control. It meant an army commander could order up several different missions at once with just a few simple orders given to different corps commanders. Without quasi-autonomous, self-orienting units tailored to grapple with any strategic situation, effective deployment of the vast resources available against the numerous threats France faced would have been impossible.

Another principle that emerged from the rapid military reorganization of the 1790s was that of multilevel staffing to control the self-sufficient horizontally articulated units. Very large regiments were unwieldy for maneuver, so instead of increasing their size, the innovators grouped them together and added a higher level of command to coordinate them. The regimental staff, however, was not eliminated. This principle was followed at ever-higher levels, so that when Napoleon inherited the army, there were many levels of staffs. These staff commanders coordinated the actions of ever larger numbers of troops. This was done, however, without greatly enlarging the regiment at the bottom, which was already of an efficient size.

French organizers did not change or eliminate the regiment but instead found they had to keep adding ever-loftier echelons between the regiment and the overall commander, who represented the state. By 1804, one of Napoleon's armies enjoyed the services of Napoleon's army staff, corps staffs, division staffs, and regimental staffs. Field armies operating on other frontiers had in addition their army staffs that were subordinate to Napoleon's staff.

Multilevel staffing and quasi-autonomous, self-sufficient formations at all levels brought important benefits. Without this carefully articulated command structure, Napoleon's guiding of an undifferentiated mass of a million men for strategic goals would have been impossible. With the multilevel command structure, however, this system was remarkably responsive. Napoleon could give a simple order describing the strategic objective, and tens of thousands of persons would begin toiling in complex ways to see to it that the objective was reached, each attending to that part of the complicated mission that he knew about and cared about.

A degree of operational freedom was given to corps commanders, and sometimes to lower echelon commanders, to exercise initiative in implementation. Regiments (and also units at other levels) vied with each other for "glory," that is, recognition from Napoleon and from the French public. If one unit discovered a better way to do something, others would quickly emulate it. There was redundancy at all levels. If a regiment's morale broke, another could be sent in. In sum, this new system, although ostensibly monolithic under the emperor's will, nevertheless had many of the attributes usually associated with pluralism: competition among units, lower-level initiative with respect to means, redundancy, and the independent quest for superior methods. The invention of the new system, with multilevel staffs and horizontally articulated units at all levels, was what made this pluralist flexibility possible. Implicit in all this was the principle of unity of strategic ends linked to a supple pluralism in implementational means: unity of ends, plurality of means.

Napoleon did not invent any of these new organizational practices of the 1790s. Instead, these changes took place while Napoleon was still a young officer. Napoleon is nevertheless closely associated with the new organizations by historians because he employed them so successfully later in the field. This brings us to another essential feature of strategic organization that emerged in the Napoleonic decades: the so-called general staff, that is, the new system for deploying strategic assets at the highest level. In the French army, Napoleon was the system. His adversaries referred to him as "the genius," among less flattering epithets.[12] Napoleon had a headquarters staff of 400 officers who acted as little more that a clerical staff, however, seeing to it that Napoleon's decisions were implemented and attending to the details of the army's logistics. Napoleon had exceptional capabilities as a commander. Before campaigning, indeed before declaring war, he read voraciously everything he could about his adversary and developed thorough plans for the campaign, with many branches and sequels to accommodate the unexpected.[13] Napoleon's adversaries did not have a dominating genius in their midst like Napoleon, however, nor did they necessarily want one.

The Prussian army at the time, stressed by repeated humiliations and defeats at Napoleon's hands, created an institution to do what the lonely genius did, namely to achieve complete conceptual mastery over strategic situations and to make the best possible plans and decisions for strategic deployment. The most-talented persons in the army were carefully selected and formed into a permanent elite staff whose purpose was to develop plans for strategic deployment of the force and to supervise their implementation. This institution, of course, was the general staff. It was conceived by Scharnhorst and the talented circle around him. Put into place during the Prussian military reforms of 1813, the general staff played a role in the campaigns of 1813 and 1815, the only campaigns in which Prussian arms proved competitive with Napoleon.

The institution of the general staff was eventually adopted by most other modern services. In a modern army effective and reliable deployment of assets on a strategic scale requires a dedicated and talented staff, a "general staff," to make plans and supervise implementation of them. The general staff translates the public will into usable plans. The institution itself functions as the strategic genius that guides operations, that serves in effect as the functional equivalent of Napoleon himself.

What do all these Napoleonic institutional arrangements have to do with twentieth-century Japan? Modern strategic organization has a number of attributes: It is subject to the public will, uses public resources, is guided by a single strategic will and purpose as developed by a professional staff at the highest level, and is implemented through an elaborate, permanent multilevel staff structure with many self-sufficient units implementing policy autonomously at the lower operational levels. Virtually all of these attributes appear for the first time among major European powers in the Napoleonic era, between 1789 and 1815.

Japan's twentieth-century postwar economy appears to impose some of these dynamic attributes of modern strategic organization on its techno-industrial system. Relatively little in the upper echelons of Japanese economic organization is entirely original conceptually. Much of it is a commonplace of modern strategic organization, which historians might trace, with some justification, to the early nineteenth century. Commentators do not usually speak of Japan as a Napoleonic economy, but they might in some respects be justified in doing so.

Adam Smith: Public Participation

These several perspectives of Schumpeter, List, and Napoleon provide insights into the nature of strategic economy. Most of Japan's economic system, however, is quotidian, and not strategic at all. Most of Japan's economy is private and commercial. The Japanese public seems to have decided to conceptualize certain industrial operations as being in the nature of public activity and to have developed certain institutional mechanisms to coordinate and accommodate these selected industries. The Japanese public has nevertheless chosen to leave most economic activity outside this rubric, and still to regard it as private and commercial in nature. This raises an interesting question: How do Japanese leaders determine which economic activities have an importance that justifies public participation, and which not? If no activities were brought under public sponsorship, there would be no economic miracle, and if too many were brought under public sponsorship, it might lead to an unwelcome rigidity. Adam Smith provided persuasive arguments in his *Wealth of Nations* (1776) as to why all manner of economic activities should be left to private interests. Smith is thus the theorist who can provide compelling justification for the large, private, quotidian sector in a strategic economy. Smith can do more for us than this, however. In exploring the limits of the private, Smith logically enough also explored the limits of the public. He developed a set of ideas to explain where the boundary between public and private should properly lie, precisely the kind of rationale that might be needed to address the question of what should be brought under policy sponsorship and what not.

In his Book 5, Smith described several important but especially challenging activities that should be left to "the sovereign or commonwealth." The first of these was external defense. "The first duty of the sovereign, that of protecting the society from the violence and invasion of other independent societies, can be performed only by means of a military force. ... When the art of war too has gradually grown up to be a very ... complicated science, ... it becomes universally necessary that the public should maintain those who serve the public in war." Smith explained that under contemporary circumstances, a trained standing army had become necessary for successful defense against invasion. The expense of this had become so great that only the commonwealth could realistically bear it.[14]

Smith went on: "The second duty of the sovereign" is "protecting ... every member of the society from the injustice or oppression of every other member of it, or the duty of establishing an exact administration of justice." Smith had in mind an impartial magistracy, paid by the crown but independent of it. This was because "the liberty of every individual, the sense which he has of his own security" depended "upon the impartial administration of justice."[15]

Smith's commonwealth had yet another duty:

> The third duty of the ... commonwealth is that of erecting and maintaining those public institutions and those public works, which, though they be in the highest degree advantageous to a great society, are, however, of such a nature, that the profit could never repay the expense to any individual or small number of individuals. ... After the ... public works necessary for the defence of the society ... the other works and institutions of this kind are chiefly those for facilitating the commerce of the society...

Smith had in mind "good roads, bridges, navigable canals, harbors" and the like. Smith rounded out his Book 5 with a few more salutary tasks for the commonwealth, such as providing for education.[16]

Smith's instincts about government were definitely minimalist. Despite this, he offered several major categories of things that modern circumstances obliged governments to do. Our times differ from Smith's times, and Japanese leaders may not be motivated by an awareness of Smith. What is interesting to note here, however, is that if one considers the kinds of benefits that accrue to Japan from strategic-economic practices, and that Japanese leaders are evidently striving to achieve by such practices, they do not fall too far from Smith's strict categories. Strategic-economic practices do for Japan more or less what Smith said government was supposed to do for society. Strategic economy is an important pillar of international security. The resources it creates constitute influence in themselves. Moreover, modern military defense depends perhaps more than anything else on advanced armaments and equipment, which strategic economy also potentially provides.

In addition strategic economy seems to have a welfarist effect and a welfarist purpose. It fosters a degree of prosperity and thus also social content and civil peace. Growing prosperity for all, linked closely to productive employments, provides a measure of distributive justice. This is a little different from Smith's "administration of justice," which mainly regulated relations among individuals. The welfarist dimension of strategic economy does, however, like Smith's administration of justice, have the effect of minimizing disorderly and unlawful conduct and thereby ensuring domestic security.

Under modern conditions, certain essential industries, such as railroads, amount to public works: They provide widespread commercial opportunities that invigorate all private commerce, and although their benefits may far outweigh the investment required, the vast funds needed to first establish such industries may be beyond what any probable combination of private interests might be likely to assemble. The availability of a large volume of inexpensive steel may invigorate a wide range of other industries, for example, and indeed may be necessary to their success. Microprocessors are a more recent instance. It is true that Smith never advocated government participation in modern industries. He did accept government participation in high roads, bridges, canals, harbors, and the like under some circumstances, however, for reasons that seem not too different from those of Japanese leaders when they choose to bring certain selected industrial activities under public sponsorship.

Adam Smith provides an explanation of why laissez-faire should be allowed to prevail in the broad nonstrategic zones of an economy. Moreover, although he does not present a definitive basis for deciding where to draw the boundary between strategic and nonstrategic zones, he does offer some plausible criteria for establishing such a boundary. These criteria may provide a point of departure in the Western scholarly tradition for trying to explain Japanese conduct in this area.

There is very little in Japanese economic practice that cannot be comprehended if one searches the rich, vast treasury of Western learning. One may, however, need to look in several unexpected places in the West's great philosophical storehouse. Much of Japanese practice, in any case, may be grasped with reference to Schumpeter, List, Napoleon, and Smith. Schumpeter anticipates the deliberate combination of interventionist and noninterventionist elements. List explains the importance of production for domestic and international economic action. Events of the Napoleonic era help illustrate the structural dynamics of the Japanese system. Smith may provide insights into why some economic activities are brought within the system's ambit and some not.

Commentators who attempt to describe all of Japan's economic activity in terms of conventional private commerce alone may find themselves offering exceptions. Many Japanese economic practices can be described more simply just by assuming that those practices resemble public institutional activity in the West, meaning the activity of academic, diplomatic, national security, or other public institutional environments. Recognizing that a significant portion of Japan's economy may constitute a strategic-economic system may of itself makes Japanese economic activity rather easier to understand. Doing so may make a thousand marvelous details of the Japanese system, otherwise so unexpected and miraculous, seem instead to be relatively ordinary and predictable.

Certain techno-industrial and financial activities in Japan appear to have been brought under a kind of public sponsorship. Resourceful recent scholarship is increasingly bringing various attributes of this arrangement to light. Many useful insights into it can be achieved by examining the system itself, as we have seen, and by exploring the abundant Western literature on political economy, on strategic organization, and on the appropriate conditions for public participation in a modern society's various activities.

Notes

1. Joseph A. Schumpeter, *Capitalism, Socialism and Democracy* (New York: Harper and Row, 1975 [1942]), pp. 167–68.

2. Ibid., pp. 131–33, 175–77, 195.

3. Ibid., pp. 173–75, 179-82, 184.

4. On Schumpeter and Japan, cf. also Thomas K. McCraw, "Schumpeter Ascending," *American Scholar* (Sum 91): 371–92, pp. 375, 389, 390.

5. Frederick List, *National System of Political Economy*, G. A. Matile trans. (Philadelphia: Lippincott, 1856 [1841]), pp. 191, 194, 222, 232–33, 262; Friedrich List, *The Natural System of Political Economy*, W. O. Henderson trans. (London: Frank Cass, 1983 [1837]), p. 181.

6. These are List's words, quoted by Roman Szporluk, *Communism and Nationalism: Karl Marx Versus Friedrich List* (New York: Oxford University Press, 1988), p. 115. Szporluk offers many useful insights into List's thought. See also List, *National System*, pp. 211– 12.

7. List, *National System*, pp. 246, 341; List, *Natural System*, pp. 101–02.

8. List, *National System*, p. 375; List, *Natural System*, p. 35.

9. List, *National System*, p. 262; List, *Natural System*, p. 178.

10. These insights and words of List are gathered in W. O. Henderson's thoughtful introduction. See List, *Natural System*, p. 6.

11. List, *National System*, p. 238; List, *Natural System*, p. 32.

12. Napoleon was probably the model for Clausewitz's account of the military "genius," the commander of "exceptional achievements." See Carl Von Clausewitz, *On War* (Princeton, NJ: Princeton University Press, 1984 [1833]), pp. 100–12.

13. David G. Chandler, *The Campaigns of Napoleon* (New York: Macmillan, 1966), p. 145.

14. Adam Smith, *The Wealth of Nations* (Chicago: University of Chicago, 1976 [1776]), pp. 213, 217, 213–31 passim.

15. Ibid., pp. 231, 244, 231-44 passim.

16. Ibid., pp. 244, 245, 244-82 passim.

Acronyms

BOJ	Bank of Japan
CIA	Central Intelligence Agency (U.S.)
EIBJ	Export Import Bank of Japan
EPA	Economic Planning Agency
FBI	Federal Bureau of Investigation (U.S.)
FILP	Fiscal Investment and Loan Plan
GATT	General Agreement on Tariffs and Trade (A global trade treaty and its supervisory apparatus)
GDP	Gross Domestic Product
IBM	International Business Machines
ISC	Industrial Structure Council
JCCI	Japan Chamber of Commerce and Industry
JDB	Japan Development Bank
JECC	Japan Electronic Computer Company
JETRO	Japan External Trade Organization
JFTC	Japan Fair Trade Commission
KGB	Principal intelligence agency of recently dissolved Soviet Union
LDP	Liberal Democratic Party
LIPCO	Livestock Industry Promotion Corporation
MIIB	Machine and Information Industries Bureau
MITI	Ministry of International Trade and Industry
MOF	Ministry of Finance
NAMC	Nippon Aircraft Manufacturing Company
NEC	Nippon Electric Company
NYK	Nihon Yusen Kaisha (Japan Mail Steamship Company)
NTT	Nippon Telephone and Telegraph
OECF	Overseas Economic Cooperation Fund
PPC	Public policy company

PSS   Postal Savings System
TDK   Toyo Denki Kaisha (Oriental Electric Company)
TRW   U.S.-based manufacturing corporation
VLSI   Very Large Scale Integration Development Association (Agency for
          development of integrated circuit technology)

Glossary

Bank of Japan	Central bank, under supervisory authority of the Ministry of Finance
Cartel	A group of companies fashioned to carry out a specific task and dismantled when that task is completed
City Banks	Twelve banks licensed to operate in major Japanese cities, including six neo-zaibatsu main banks
Export Councils	An association of corporations in the same industry whose purpose is to facilitate export
Foreign Exchange and Trade Control Law	Comprehensive law to control flows of funds and materials into and out of Japan
General Trading Companies	Ten corporations that handle largescale international commodities trading and other overseas functions for the respective neo-zaibatsu groups
Industrial Associations	Industry-wide group of companies that implements tasks requiring homogeneity of function among firms
Industrial Structure Council	Body that advises MITI on economic policy
Japan External Trade Organization	MITI agency that gathers strategic-economic intelligence abroad
Japan Fair Trade Commission	Agency that registers public policy cartels and prosecutes cartels that are not authorized.
Machinary and Information Industries Bureau	MITI bureau that oversees high value-added production of machinery, electronic and optical goods, computer goods, and vehicles

Ministry of International Trade and Industry	Ministry supervising Japan's economic strategies at home and abroad: "Economic general staff"
Mundane Economy	That part of the economy engaged in quotidian consumer activity. This sector embraces between a half and three-quarters of all non-governmental economic activity.
Neo-Zaibatsu	Six groups of approximately 30 companies each that implement strategic tasks requiring diversity of capability among firms
Overseas Economic Cooperation Fund	MITI body that lends to foreign countries in support of development projects carried out by Japanese corporations in those countries.
Postal Savings System	A consumer banking service operated by the Japanese postal system
Presidents' Club	Group consisting of the presidents of member firms of a neo-zaibatsu. Normally convenes once a month.
Public Policy Companies	Semi-autonomous agencies that carry out particular public functions, including serving as passthrough monopoly companies that determine the price and flow of certain strategic commodities
Regional Banks	Approximately 64 banks licensed to operate outside major cities
Satellite Corporation	Corporation whose policies are entirely or partially determined by a strategic corporation, usually through a controlling stock interest
Strategic Corporation	One of about 200 premier corporations that carry out strategic manufacturing, financing, and services
Strategic Economy	That part of the economy engaged in strategic production, financing, and services. This sector embraces between a quarter and a half of all non-governmental economic activity.

Bibliography

Abegglen, James C. "The Economic Growth of Japan." *Scientific American* 222.3 (Mar 70): 31–37.

_____. *Management and Worker.* Tokyo: Sophia University, 1973.

Abegglen, James C., and Stalk, George. *Kaisha.* New York: Basic Books, 1985.

Anchordoguy, Marie. *Computers, Inc.: Japan's Challenge to IBM.* Cambridge, MA: Harvard Council on East Asian Studies, 1989.

Anderson, Stephen J. "The Political Economy of Japanese Saving." *Journal of Japanese Studies* 16.1 (Win 90): 61–92.

Blumenthal, Tuvia. "The Japanese Shipbuilding Industry." Pp. 129–60 in Hugh Patrick ed. *Japanese Industrialization and Its Social Consequences.*

Borrus, Michael, Millstein, James, and Zysman, John. *U.S.-Japanese Competition in the Semiconductor Industry.* Berkeley, CA: Institute of International Relations, 1982.

Boxer, Charles R. *The Portuguese Seaborne Empire, 1415–1825.* London: Hutchinson, 1969.

Calder, Kent E. "Linking Welfare and the Developmental State: Postal Savings in Japan." *Journal of Japanese Studies* 16.1 (Win 90): 31–59.

Caves, Richard E., and Uekusa, Masu. "Industrial Organization." Pp. 459–523 in Hugh Patrick and Henry Rosovsky eds. *Asia's New Giant.*

_____. *Industrial Organization in Japan.* Washington, DC: Brookings Institution, 1976.

Chandler, Alfred D. *Strategy and Structure.* Cambridge, MA: MIT Press, 1962.

Chandler, David G. *The Campaigns of Napoleon.* New York: Macmillan, 1966.

Choate, Pat. *Agents of Influence.* New York: Alfred A. Knopf, 1990.

Clark, Rodney. *The Japanese Company.* New Haven: Yale University Press, 1979.

Clausewitz, Carl Von. *On War.* Michael Howard and Peter Paret trans. Princeton, NJ: Princeton University Press, 1984 [1833].

Cole, Robert E. *Japanese Blue Collar.* Berkeley, CA: University of California Press, 1971.

Corporate Disclosure in Japan: Reporting. The Japanese Institute of Certified Public Accountants ed. Tokyo: JICPA, 1984.

Dore, Ronald. *British Factory–Japanese Factory.* Berkeley: University of California Press, 1973.

_____. *Taking Japan Seriously: A Confucian Perspective on Leading Economic Issues.* Stanford, CA: Stanford University Press, 1987.

Drifte, Reinhard. *Arms Production in Japan.* Boulder, CO: Westview Press, 1986.

Field Manual 100–5: Operations. Headquarters Department of the Army ed. Washington, DC: USGPO, 1986.

Freeman, Christopher. *Technology Policy and Economic Performance: Lessons from Japan.* London: Pinter, 1987.

Fruin, W. Mark. "Instead of Management: Internal Contracting and the Genesis of Modern Labor Relations." Pp. 109–34 in Tsunehiko Yui et al. eds. *Japanese Management in Historical Perspective.*

_____. *The Japanese Enterprise System.* New York: Oxford University Press, 1992.

Fukui, Haruhiro. "Economic Planning in Postwar Japan." *Asian Survey* 12.4 (Apr 72): 327–48.

Gerlach, Michael. *Alliance Capitalism.* Berkeley, CA: University of California Press, 1992.

_____. "*Keiretsu* Organization in the Japanese Economy." Pp. 141–74 in C. Johnson, L. Tyson, and J. Zysman eds., *Politics and Productivity.*

_____. "Twilight of the *Keiretsu?* A Critical Assessment." *Journal of Japanese Studies* 18:1 (Win 92): 79–118.

Gordon, Andrew. *The Evolution of Labor Relations in Japan.* Cambridge, MA: Harvard Council on East Asian Studies, 1985.

Hadley, Eleanor M. *Antitrust in Japan.* Princeton, NJ: Princeton University Press, 1970.

Hart, B. H. Liddell. *Strategy.* New York: Meridian, 1991 [1954].

Hollerman, Leon. *Japan's Economic Strategy in Brazil.* Lexington, MA: Lexington-Heath, 1988.

Huber, Thomas M. "Men of High Purpose." Pp. 107–27 in Tetsuo Najita and J. Victor Koschmann eds., *Conflict in Modern Japanese History.* Princeton, NJ: Princeton University Press, 1982.

Japan Statistical Yearbook. Statistics Bureau ed. Tokyo: Japan Statistical Association, 1988.

Johnson, Chalmers. "Japan: Who Governs?" *Journal of Japanese Studies* 2.1 (Aut 75): 1–28.

_____. *Japan's Public Policy Companies.* Washington, DC: American Enterprise Institute, 1978.

_____. *MITI and the Japanese Miracle.* Stanford, CA: Stanford University Press, 1982.

_____. "MITI, MPT, and the Telecom Wars." Pp. 177–240 in C. Johnson, L. Tyson, and J. Zysman eds., *Politics and Productivity.*

Johnson, Chalmers, Tyson, Laura D'Andrea, and Zysman, John eds. *Politics and Productivity.* New York: Ballinger, 1989.

Jomini, Antoine Henri de. *The Art of War.* Novato, CA: Presidio Press, 1992.

_____. *Summary of the Art of War.* Pp. 432–557 in Stackpole Books ed., *Roots of Strategy, Book 2.* Harrisburg, PA: Stackpole Books, 1987.

Kenrick, Douglas M. *The Success of Competitive Communism in Japan.* London: Macmillan, 1988.

Kondratieff, Nikolai D. *The Long Wave Cycle.* New York: Richardson and Snyder, 1984 [1925].

Lincoln, Edward J. *Japan's Unequal Trade.* Washington, DC: The Brookings Institution, 1990.

List, Frederick. *The National System of Political Economy.* G. A. Matile trans. Philadelphia: Lippincott, 1856 [1841].

――――. *The Natural System of Political Economy.* W. O. Henderson trans. London: Frank Cass, 1983 [1837].

Luttwak, Edward N. *Strategy: The Logic of War and Peace.* Cambridge, MA: Belknap Press, 1987.

Lynn, Leonard, and McKeown, Timothy J. *Organizing Business: Trade Associations in America and Japan.* Washington, DC: American Enterprise Institute, 1988.

Magaziner, Ira C., and Hout, Thomas M. *Japanese Industrial Policy.* Berkeley, CA: Institute of International Studies, 1980.

McCraw, Thomas K. "Schumpeter Ascending." *American Scholar* (Sum 91): 371–92.

McMillan, Charles J. *The Japanese Industrial System.* Berlin: Walter de Gruyter, 1984.

Minami, Ryoshin. *The Economic Development of Japan.* London: Macmillan Press, 1986.

Murata, Kiyoji, and Ota, Isamu eds. *An Industrial Geography of Japan.* London: Bell and Hyman, 1980.

Nishiyama, Tadanori. "The Structure of Managerial Control: Who Owns and Controls Japanese Businesses?" Pp. 123–63 in Kazuo Sato and Yasuo Hoshino eds., *The Anatomy of Japanese Business.*

Organization for Economic Cooperation and Development. *The Industrial Policy of Japan.* Paris: OECD, 1972.

Ozaki, Robert S. *The Control of Imports and Foreign Capital in Japan.* New York: Praeger, 1972.

Patrick, Hugh ed. *Japanese Industrialization and Its Social Consequences.* Berkeley: University of California Press, 1976.

Patrick, Hugh, and Rosovsky, Henry eds. *Asia's New Giant.* Washington, DC: Brookings Institution, 1976.

Pechman, Joseph A. "Taxation." Pp. 317–82 in Hugh Patrick and Henry Rosovsky eds., *Asia's New Giant.*

Pempel, T. J. "Japanese Foreign Economic Policy: The Domestic Bases for International Behavior." Pp. 723–74 in Peter J. Katzenstein ed., *Between Power and Plenty: Foreign Economic Policies of Advanced Industrial Countries.* Published as a special edition of *International Organization* 31.4 (Aut 77): 581–920 (whole volume).

Prestowitz, Clyde V. *Trading Places.* New York: Basic Books, 1988.

Richelson, Jeffrey T. *Foreign Intelligence Organizations.* Cambridge, MA: Ballinger, 1988.

Rohlen, Thomas P. *For Harmony and Strength.* Berkeley, CA: University of California Press, 1974.

Samuels, Richard J., and Whipple, Benjamin C. "Defense Production and Industrial Development: The Case of Japanese Aircraft." Pp. 275–318 in C. Johnson, L. Tyson, and J. Zysman eds., *Politics and Productivity.*

Sato, Kazuo, and Hoshino, Yasuo eds. *The Anatomy of Japanese Business.* Armonk, NY: M. E. Sharpe, 1984.

Schumpeter, Joseph A. *Capitalism, Socialism and Democracy.* New York: Harper and Row, 1975 [1942].

Scott, James C. *Domination and the Arts of Resistance.* New Haven, CT: Yale University Press, 1990.

Shinohara, Miyohei. *Industrial Growth, Trade, and Dynamic Patterns in the Japanese Economy.* Tokyo: University of Tokyo Press, 1982.

Smith, Adam. *The Wealth of Nations.* Chicago: University of Chicago, 1976 [1776].

Smith, Thomas C. *Native Sources of Japanese Industrialization, 1750–1920.* Berkeley, CA: University of California Press, 1988.

Subrahmanyam, Sanjay. *The Portuguese Empire in Asia 1500–1700: A Political and Economic History.* London: Longmans, 1992.

Sun Tzu. *The Art of Strategy.* R. L. Wing trans. New York: Doubleday, 1988.

––––––. *The Art of War.* Samuel B. Griffith trans. London: Oxford University Press, 1963.

Suzuki, Yoshio ed. *Japan's Financial System.* Oxford: Oxford University Press, 1987.

Suzuki, Yoshio. *Money, Finance, and Macroeconomic Performance in Japan.* New Haven, CT: Yale University Press, 1986.

Szporluk, Roman. *Communism and Nationalism: Karl Marx Versus Friedrich List.* New York: Oxford University Press, 1988.

Totten, George O. "The Great Noda Strike of 1927–1928." Pp. 398–436 in Bernard S. Silberman et al. eds., *Japan in Crisis.* Princeton, NJ: Princeton University Press, 1974.

Trezise, Philip H., and Suzuki, Yukio. "Politics, Government, and Economic Growth in Japan." Pp. 753–811 in Hugh Patrick and Henry Rosovsky eds., *Asia's New Giant.*

Tsusan handobukku [*MITI Handbook*]. Tsusan handobukku henshu iinkai ed. [MITI Handbook Editing Committee ed.] Tokyo: Shokokaikan, 1989.

Tsusho sangyo roppo [*International Trade and Industry Laws*]. Tsusho sangyo-sho ed. [MITI ed.] Tokyo: Marui Kobunsha, 1988.

Vogel, Ezra F. *Japan as Number One.* New York: Harper and Row, 1979.

Wolf, Marvin J. *The Japanese Conspiracy.* New York: Empire Books, 1983.

Wolferen, Karel Van. *The Enigma of Japanese Power.* New York: Alfred A. Knopf, 1989.

Yasuba, Yasukichi. "The Evolution of Dualistic Wage Structure." Pp. 249–98 in Hugh Patrick ed., *Japanese Industrialization and Its Social Consequences.*

Yoshihara, Kunio. *Sogo Shosha: The Vanguard of the Japanese Economy.* New York: Oxford University Press, 1982.

Young, Alexander K. *The Sogo Shosha: Japan's Multinational Trading Companies.* Boulder, CO: Westview Press, 1979.

Yui, Tsunehiko et al. ed. *Japanese Management in Historical Perspective.* Tokyo: University of Tokyo Press, 1989.

Zysman, John. *Governments, Markets, and Growth.* Ithaca, NY: Cornell University Press, 1983.

About the Book and Author

THIS INNOVATIVE WORK demystifies the Japanese economy by considering it as a strategic system. Showing how the Japanese "miracle" is actively planned, directed, and implemented by a constellation of institutions, government policymakers, and big business, Huber argues that Japan, Inc., can best be compared to a modern military system rather than exclusively to a free-market economy. The author highlights particularly the similarity between Japan's strategic economy and some of the structures and policy dynamics of the U.S. military and shows how Japan's economic strategies have the capability of adversely affecting its trading partners.

Thomas M. Huber is an institutional historian and Japan specialist on the history faculty of the Army graduate school in Fort Leavenworth, Kansas (U.S. Army Command and General Staff College). He received his Ph.D. in history from the University of Chicago and has served as a visiting assistant professor in the history departments of Stanford University, the University of California–Berkeley, and other major universities. His earlier publications include *The Revolutionary Origins of Modern Japan* (1981).

Index